CONTENTS

Chapter One: Homelessness in the UK

Chapter Two: Seeking Solutions

Introduction

The Plight of the Homeless is the fiftieth volume in the **Issues** series. The aim of this series is to offer up-to-date information about important issues in our world.

The Plight of the Homeless looks at the problems confronting the homeless and what is being done to resolve the situation.

The information comes from a wide variety of sources and includes:
Government reports and statistics
Newspaper reports and features
Magazine articles and surveys
Literature from lobby groups
and charitable organisations.

It is hoped that, as you read about the many aspects of the issues explored in this book, you will critically evaluate the information presented. It is important that you decide whether you are being presented with facts or opinions. Does the writer give a biased or an unbiased report? If an opinion is being expressed, do you agree with the writer?

The Plight of the Homeless offers a useful starting-point for those who need convenient access to information about the many issues involved. However, it is only a starting-point. At the back of the book is a list of organisations which you may want to contact for further information.

*****

Questions and answers on homelessness

Information from Catholic Housing Aid Society (CHAS)

CHAS gets many letters from pupils asking questions about our work and homelessness in general. Here, answering many of those questions, Rosie Hughes from St Mary's School, London, interviews CHAS Outreach Officer, Jennie Richmond.

Q: Can you tell me how many people are homeless in this country?
A: That depends on what you mean by 'homeless'.

Q: Huh?
A: Think of all the things you associate with a home. Somewhere that is warm and dry. Somewhere where you are welcome and can belong. Where you can sleep and eat, work or just do nothing. A place that is safe and secure. Where you can keep your belongings. Where you can invite friends to visit. That's a home. A home is far more than a roof over your head. It is a place where people can meet their physical needs like warmth and safety, but also where they can grow as people,

finding security and space. People are homeless or in housing need if they do not have a decent, secure and affordable home.

Q: So who is homeless then?
A: Many people imagine that the only people who are homeless are those who live on the streets, so-called rough sleepers. But if home means more than a roof over your head, are you not 'homeless' without those things? The government divides homeless people into two categories – 'statutorily' and 'non-statutorily' homeless.

Q: What does that mean? What's the difference?
A: It's quite complicated, but basically statutorily homeless people are people that local authorities are obliged to help by law – or statute – and so they are the only ones who are counted by the government. To qualify for help under the homelessness legislation – in other words to be statutorily homeless – you have to jump through a number of hoops.

You have to be:
- homeless,
- not intentionally homeless,
- 'in priority need' (which means that the household has to include children, old people, a pregnant woman or someone who is equally vulnerable)
- and 'eligible for assistance' which, for instance, excludes most people from abroad seeking asylum

As a result most single people and childless couples do not qualify as statutorily homeless, and so do not receive any help.

Q: OK, so if you are statutorily homeless, what help do you get?
A: Under new legislation the local authority has a duty to house statutorily homeless people in temporary accommodation for two years at a time.

Q: Only temporary accommodation?
A: Yes. Which often causes a lot of problems in itself. For example a family may face frequent moves around, sometimes only staying in

the same place for a few weeks or months. Children may have to keep moving schools, losing contact with their friends and falling behind with their work; parents may have to give up their jobs; families have to keep re-registering with doctors, dentists, benefit offices, employment offices and so on.

Q: But what about the people who don't qualify as homeless under the law?
A: They're called non-statutorily homeless. This category is a huge one and includes everyone who is not considered to be 'in priority need'. Local authorities are not obliged to help these people even though they might be sleeping rough, living in hostels or in bed and breakfast, sleeping on friends' floors, living in overcrowded housing or in insecure or dangerous accommodation, trapped in violent situations or seeking asylum.

Q: So what help do homeless people who aren't in priority need get?
A: Local authorities have a duty to provide 'advice and assistance', but this kind of help is often not sufficient to help people who need secure and affordable homes. Many homeless people have to rely on charity or the goodwill of friends.

Q: So that's where CHAS and other agencies come in?
A: That's right. Together, we work to directly help those in housing need, as well as working to try to prevent the conditions that lead to homelessness.

• The above information is an extract from CHAS's web site which can be found at www.chasnat.demon.co.uk/
© CHAS

Homelessness – the facts

Information from the National Homeless Alliance

It would be impossible to give a total number of all homeless people in the UK for a number of reasons. Firstly, there are many different ways of defining someone as 'homeless' – for instance people may be sleeping rough, squatting, living on a friend's floor or living in short-hold insecure tenancies.

Secondly, getting statistics which cover the wide range of situations people find themselves in is very difficult. Some, but not all, local authorities conduct counts of rough sleepers on a particular night, but this only really gives an idea of the scale of the problem rather than an accurate figure. Other figures can be obtained by surveys, research or government statistics. However, if people do not come into contact with statutory or voluntary services they can remain 'hidden' from official figures.

The true extent of the problem can only be estimated, but it is important to keep an eye on the situation in order to gauge the success or failure of service provision and government policies.

Local authority figures
The Department of the Environ-ment, Transport and the Regions produces quarterly bulletins giving detailed information on home-lessness. These statistics are collected from local authorities and only cover those people who have approached the authority for help and are eligible for housing under the 1996 Housing Act. The figures show the number of households, not necessarily individuals.

Local authorities have slightly differing eligibility criteria for accepting people as intentionally or unintentionally homeless and whe-ther they are in 'priority' need. There are guidelines set out in the 1996 Act and subsequent documents. Broadly speaking, priority need only

...DO WE FIT THE DEFINITION OF HOMELESS?

...GOT NOTHING THAT FITS THE DEFINITION OF HOME-SWEET-HOME...

SK

covers families (i.e. where there are children involved) and other specific cases. The extent of single homeless-ness is therefore not covered.

• In 1998 in England, there were 166,430 households accepted as homeless. Of these:
• 105,840 were classified as unintentionally homeless and in priority need;
• 6,120 intentionally homeless and in priority need and;
• 54,470 homeless and not in priority need.
• In 1998 27% lost their home because friends or relatives could no longer accommodate them, 24% because of relationship breakdown, and 6% because of mortgage arrears.

Temporary accommodation
The numbers of households in temporary accommodation arranged by their local authority in 1998:
• 193,890 in total of which;
• 22,000 were in B&B hotels;
• 36,950 were in hostels or women's refuges;
• 60,430 were in private sector accommodation;
• 74,510 in 'other' accommodation (housing association or local authority stock).
Source: The Department of the Environment, Transport and the

Regions (DETR). Tel: 020 7890 3333. Web site: www.detr.gov.uk

Single homelessness

There are no comprehensive or reliable figures for single homelessness nationally due to the complexities of the situation and any figure would have to include single people in hostels and B&Bs, rough sleepers, squatters, etc.

- 28,353 households accepted by local authorities as homeless in 1996/97 had a single occupant.
- A report by the London Research Centre in 1996 estimated there to be over 100,000 single homeless people in London.

Further information: Isobel Anderson, Peter A. Kemp and Deborah Quilgars (1993) *Single Homeless People*, London: HMSO. Produced by the University of York for the DETR. Web site: www.york.ac.uk/inst/chp/homeless.htm

Rough sleeping

The government has recently produced the first official national estimate of the extent of rough sleeping in England. This was based on local authority counts and estimates, but many authorities did not provide any statistics. There are no definitive and robust figures to rely on, due to the transient nature of the population.

- In June 1998, the DETR estimated there to be 1,850 people sleeping rough on any given night in England. Of these, 621 were in London.
- A report by Shelter in 1997 gave an estimate that in England outside London 2,000 sleep rough each night and 10,000 people drift in and out of rough sleeping over the course of a year.
- An estimate by the Housing Services Agency in 1998 gave a figure of 400 on any given night in London and 2,400 throughout the year.
- In Scotland in 1995, there were estimates from 4,231 to 5,798 rough sleepers.

Further information: Social Exclusion Unit, *Rough Sleepers Report*. Tel: 020 7270 5253. Web site: www.cabinet-office.gov.uk/seu/1998/rough/srhome.htm

Hostel provision

- There are 529 hostels (emergency and non-emergency) in London.
- Of these, there are around 50 emergency (direct access) hostels. These provide 3,000 bedspaces.
- Nationally there are nearly 1,900 hostels, containing around 27,000 beds, being provided or used by local authority housing departments in England.

Sources: Research Information Service, Hostels Online. Tel: 020 7494 2408. Web site: www.ris.org.uk.

The Department of the Environment, Transport and the Regions (DETR). Tel: 020 7890 3333. Web site: www.housing.detr.gov.uk/hrs/hrs050.htm

Further Information: Homeless Services Unit and the Hostels Forum, NHA. Tel: 020 7833 2071.

Squatting

Figures on the number of people squatting are very difficult to estimate. However:

- 9,600 people were estimated as squatting in England in 1995.
- 80% of squatting is thought to happen in London.

Source: London Research Centre, 1996.

Further Information: Advisory Service for Squatters. Tel: 020 7359 8814.

Bed and breakfast

The vast majority of homeless people in B&Bs are single or childless couples. Government figures only account for a small proportion of the total number due to local authority eligibility criteria and the fact that most people self-refer.

- Research by Shelter in 1996 estimates that there were 67,665 homeless people in England and Wales using B&Bs.
- 12,178 of these were in London.
- 22,000 people were placed by local authorities (see above).

Further Information: Shelter. Tel: 020 7505 2000. Web site: www.shelter.org.uk/main.html

Day centres

Day centres provide a wide range of essential services for homeless people, from food and shelter to advice and health care.

- Around 300 day centres for homeless people are currently operating in the UK.
- Day centres provide essential support for around 10,000 people every day.

Homeless households in priority need

The 1998 homeless households figures for England show a three per cent increase on 1997. However, as can be seen from the table, the general trend has been downward and the number accepted in the March quarter of 1999 (26,920) is 28 per cent lower than in the peak quarter, March 1992, when 37,190 households were accepted as being homeless and in priority need.

	1993[1]	1995[1]	1997	1998
North East	6,800	6,050	4,430	4,400
Yorkshire & Humberside	13,320	9,930	8,960	8,440
East Midlands	10,120	8,970	7,980	7,680
Eastern	9,000	8,730	8,020	8,660
London	31,570	26,690	24,850	26,480
South East	12,630	13,570	12,070	12,910
South West	9,370	9,960	8,800	9,120
West Midlands	16,440	17,510	14,500	14,180
North West	14,980	13,150	10,720	11,970
Merseyside	3,400	2,930	2,080	2,000
England	127,630	117,490	102,410	105,840
Wales	7,757[2]	5,811	4,297	4,371
Scotland[3]	19,800[4]	17,500[5]	16,800[6]	–[7]

1 Figures for 1993 and 1995 for England and Wales relate to the period when cases were dealt with under the Housing Act 1985. The data for 1997 and 1998 were dealt with under Part VII of the Housing Act 1996.
2 The figure includes an estimate of 237 households made homeless in Aberconwy as a result of the flooding incident in Llandudno during June 1993.
3 Figures for Scotland are the nearest equivalent to the English figures, under the Housing Scotland Act 1987.
4 This is the 1992/93 annual figure for Scotland.
5 This is the 1994/95 annual figure for Scotland.
6 This is the 1996/97 annual figure for Scotland.
7 Figures for 1997/98 for Scotland are not yet available.

Source: Department of the Environment Transport and the Regions Information Bulletin, March 1999. Scottish Office, Housing Trends in Scotland. Statistical Directorate 7, The National Assembly for Wales, 1999.

- Former rough sleepers make up 45% of the client base.

Source: *Saving the Day*, NHA, 1996.

Further Information: National Day Centres Project at NHA. Tel: 020 7833 2071.

Youth homelessness

Youth homelessness includes young people living on the streets and those sleeping in hostels or on friends' or relatives' floor. Care leavers are particularly vulnerable to homelessness – between a fifth and a half of all young homeless people have been in care.

- 32,100 people between the ages of 16 and 21 were estimated to be homeless in 1995 by the London Research Centre.
- A report by CHAR (now NHA) gave an estimate of 246,000 homeless people between the ages of 16 and 25 in 1995.
- 20% of homeless young people in London in 1999 had attempted suicide at least once in the past year.

- Homeless young people are twice as likely to have been physically or mentally abused.

Sources: *We didn't choose to be homeless*, CHAR, 1996. Tel: 020 7833 2071. *Health and Youth Homelessness*, Centrepoint, 1999.

Further Information: Youth Homelessness Project, NHA. Tel: 020 7833 2071. NCH Action for Children. Tel: 020 7226 2033.

Ethnic minority groups

Ethnic minority groups are over-represented in applications to housing departments and in general homelessness figures.

- 20% of the young homeless population in urban areas in 1996 were from ethnic minorities. Other national surveys have showed 31%.
- 25% of applicants for housing to local authorities in England in 1994 were from ethnic minority groups.
- 52% of applicants for housing in London in 1994 were from ethnic minority groups.

- 10% of rough sleepers in London were from black or ethnic minorities in 1998.

Sources: *Bright Lights and Homelessness*, National Council of YMCAs, 1996. *The New Picture of Youth Homelessness in Britain*, Centrepoint, 1996. *A Study of Homeless Applicants*, DETR, 1996. Homeless Network, 1998 (Tel: 020 7799 2404).

Further Information: Federation of Black Housing Organisations. Tel: 020 7388 1560.

Empty homes

- Government figures show that 753,200 homes stood empty in England in 1998.
- 111,000 of these were local authority or housing association stock.
- 623,200 were in the private sector.

Further Information: Empty Homes Agency. Tel: 020 7828 6288. Web site: www.users.globalnet.co.uk/~eha/pressrelease.htm

© National Homeless Alliance
January, 2000

Housing and homelessness in England: the facts

Shelter believes:

- A decent, safe, secure and affordable home is a basic human right.
- There is a hidden housing crisis.
- Homelessness is the result of a lack of affordable housing.
- Housing is a valuable investment, not only for the people who live in that housing, but also for their communities.

Homelessness

Homelessness is one of the most acute signs of housing shortages. In 1998, a total of 166,430 households were officially recognised as homeless by local authorities in England. Shelter estimates that this represents about 400,000 people.

This figure is only the tip of the iceberg. It does not include most of the 41,000 people who are living in hostels and squats, or the 78,000 couples or lone parents sharing accommodation who cannot afford to set up a home on their own (England and Wales).

People from minority ethnic groups are over-represented among homeless households. In 1997, 56% of households accepted as homeless by local authorities in inner London were from ethnic minorities.

Furthermore, Shelter housing advice centres around the country are reporting instances where local authorities are rehousing homeless households directly through the housing register rather than recording them as homeless applicants. This means that homelessness figures are understated and are not reflecting the real problem of homelessness and housing need.

A new Shelter report found that two-thirds of young people who sought assistance in the three areas covered in the research[1] had either slept out the night before, had nowhere to go that night or were threatened with imminent homelessness.

During 1997/98, 25% of Shelter's clients were young people under 25. Of these 80% had experienced homelessness.

Shelter estimates that around 2,000 people are sleeping on the street on any one night.

Temporary accommodation

At the end of March 1999, local authorities were housing 55,280 homeless households in temporary accommodation. Shelter research (1997) found that 76,000 people placed themselves in bed and breakfast hotels (B&Bs), because they could not find any suitable alternative accommodation. This is in addition to those homeless households placed by local authorities in B&Bs during the same period.

At the end of September 1998, there were nearly 19,000 destitute asylum seekers, including families with children, who were housed in temporary accommodation by social services in London.

Provision of social housing

Shelter estimates that an average of 115,000 affordable homes will need to have been provided between 1991 and 2011 in order to meet housing need.[2]

Housing associations are the main provider of new social housing. During 1997/98, they provided 25,370 homes to rent, this compares with 39,750 in 1993/94 (a decrease of 36%). Local authorities built only 250 homes in 1997/98.

Poor housing and empty homes

Poverty is a major barrier to obtaining good quality housing. The most economically and socially disadvantaged people in society live in the worst housing.

Over 1.9 million households (14.2%) live in poor housing. Of these, over three-quarters of a million are families with children. Nearly half a million households live in overcrowded homes.

Poor housing has an impact on health. Today there are about 400,000 households living in damp homes. Children who live in these conditions are more likely to suffer from respiratory problems, stomach upsets, fatigue and nervousness.

There are about 744,000 empty homes, 623,000 of which are in the private sector.

Access to housing

There is a shortage of good quality and affordable housing in this country. The cost of housing has been increasing ahead of inflation and average earnings.

Between 1990 and 1997, the average weekly rent in the private sector increased by nearly 85% from £45 to £83.

Between 1988/89 and 1997/98,

the average weekly rent for council housing has increased by 117% from £19.01 to £41.18. More than 1.5 million council tenants are in rent arrears.

Between 1989/90 and 1998, the cost of housing association lets increased by 110% from £24.97 to £51.67 per week.

Between 1987 and 1997, average house prices went up from nearly £40,000 to £72,900. This represents an increase of more than 80%. During 1998, a total of 33,820 owner occupiers lost their homes through repossessions.

Paying for housing

In the last two decades housing subsidy has been shifted from bricks and mortar to personal subsidies. As a result of this, the last ten years have seen gross housing investment decrease by 46% from £5,767 to £3,106 billion. At the same time the housing benefit bill has increased by 200%.

During 1998/99, 10.8 million households were receiving mortgage interest tax relief, with an estimated cost to the public purse of £1.9 billion. This tax relief is going to be phased out in April 2000.

In May 1998, a total of 4.47 million households were receiving housing benefit to help to pay for their housing at an estimated cost of about £12.2 billion. However, new research commissioned by the DETR[3] shows that 90% of private

tenants assessed for housing benefit reported shortfalls between the benefit entitlement and their rent level. Of these, 70% reported shortfalls of £10 or more per week.

In 1997/98, the total gross cost of providing temporary accommodation for homeless households was over £153 million.[4] Over £57 million of this total was spent on providing B&B accommodation.

Access denied

There are thousands of households in housing need who are denied access to social housing as a result of local authorities' practices of excluding and suspending households from the housing register. Shelter research (1998) suggested that in England as a whole around 200,000 households could have been excluded from the housing register over a two-year period (1996-1998).

References
1 Year-long monitoring via agencies in three areas – Lincolnshire, Crawley, Sheffield.
2 This figure is being revised to take account of recent household projections.
3 Department for the Environment, Transport and the Regions.
4 This figure excludes the cost of administration and welfare.

• The above information is from Shelter. See page 41 for address details.

© *Shelter*

Homelessness in Scotland

Information from Shelter – Scotland

What is homelessness?

Every night between 500 and 1,000 people sleep rough on the streets of Scotland's towns and cities.

Sleeping rough kills people. The average life expectancy for someone sleeping rough is 47 years of age. The Government has put some money into helping stop people from having to sleep rough. This is called the Rough Sleepers Initiative. The Government has stated that no-one should have to sleep rough by the year 2003. This is an ambitious target but tonight, as every night, people are facing the bleak prospect of a night spent outside.

Some people will sleep rough for just one or two nights until they find somewhere else, maybe a bed in a hostel. Others will sleep on the streets for weeks, months or even years. Some will have drug or alcohol problems, as the search for something, anything, to blot out the desperation of their reality.

Many of them will die on the streets. People freeze to death on the streets of Scotland every winter.

This is an appalling situation but it is by no means the extent of the homelessness problem. Many more people live in hostels, or in bed and breakfast hotels, too poor to buy their own home and waiting without hope for a council house or some other home.

Other people sleep on friends' couches, never sure when they will outstay their welcome, forced to live one day at a time. Families are forced to split up, mothers and children living in a relative's spare room, the father forced to stay with a friend. Normal family life is put on hold until they can find a place to be together.

And some people who count themselves lucky to have a house of their own face desperate conditions such as dampness and disrepair.

The blanket you see in a shop doorway tells just one small part of the story.

Most homeless people say they never thought homelessness could happen to them. Evidence shows that homelessness can happen to anyone, of any age and from any background.

Facts

- during 1998/99, 45,548 families and single people applied to their local council as homeless. This amounts to over 81,000 individuals;
- if all the people who were homeless last year in Scotland assembled in Scotland's largest sports stadium, Murrayfield, there would still be 13,500 locked out;
- the numbers of officially recorded homeless people in Scotland has increased by 57% in ten years;
- 80 children become homeless in Scotland every working day;
- the average life expectancy for a person living on the streets is 47 – lower than in some third world countries;
- getting a house is not always a happy ending. A quarter of council houses in Scotland are blighted with dampness and condensation.

Prevention

Prevention is better than cure. People need advice before they become homeless, as soon as it becomes clear that they have a problem. The earlier people seek help, the greater the likelihood that they will be able to stay in their homes.

Housing advice is about finding solutions to people's housing problems, preventing homelessness and enforcing people's housing rights. It can be:

- advising on a homeless person's rights to housing
- explaining the laws that enable a tenant to remain in her/his home without being harassed by the landlord
- ensuring that people receive their correct benefit entitlement to help them pay their rent
- liaising with other organisations who can offer help
- representing clients in dealings with landlords, local authorities, and housing benefit staff or
- organising a reasonable mortgage repayment package to stop a family having their home repossessed.

Why do people become homeless?

It is often said that people become homeless because of relationship breakdown or unemployment. This is not the case. Many people fact these crises in their lives but the majority will not become homeless. People become homeless because they cannot find a decent home at a price they can afford. If we are ever to solve the problem of homelessness, we need to increase the availability of good quality, low-cost rented housing.

- The above information is from Shelter – Scotland. See page 41 for address details.

© Shelter – Scotland

> *Some will have drug or alcohol problems, as the search for something, anything, to blot out the desperation of their reality*

Homelessness costs

Information from Shelter

The facts

- In 1996/97 the total gross cost of providing temporary accommodation for homeless households was over £185m. Over £51m of this total was spent on providing bed and breakfast accommodation.
- The National Health Service spends £2 billion each year treating the effects of homelessness and bad housing.

What Shelter says

Homelessness and bad housing cost individuals, society and the economy. It is time we all stopped paying the price for Britain's failed housing system.

Shelter delivers help, advice and advocacy to homeless people whilst at the same time campaigning for changes in the law. The Homelessness Costs Campaign was launched in June 1995 to drive home the message that society and individuals cannot afford to pay the price of homelessness. To raise awareness we placed adverts in the national press, the *Big Issue* and parliamentary magazines.

Shelter published important new research to draw attention to this campaign. *No Place to Learn* shows how badly children's educa-tion is affected by the constant disruption of living in temporary accommodation. *Bad for Business* explores housing problems experienced by employees and how they affect the companies they work for and the national economy. *Homelessness and Suicide* shows how homelessness and bad housing often cut people off from their family, friends, GPs and social services. You can order Shelter publications.

The issue

As individuals homeless people pay a heavy price for Britain's failed housing system – the daily horrors of insecurity, squalor, disruption to jobs and education, damage to family life

and ill health. But there is a cost to society too. Homelessness and bad housing cost the health service, education, social services and the economy in wasted resources and wasted opportunities.

- ***Housing***: The money that is spent on housing people in temporary accommodation, hostels and B&Bs could be better spent on creating permanent, safe, decent, secure and affordable homes.
- ***Jobs***: Providing homes creates jobs. A £2 billion investment in building and renovating new homes could create 30,000 jobs. Shelter believes that at least 150,000 new homes need to be provided each year for the next ten years to meet housing need. It would be better to put unemployed builders back to work and put homeless people into the permanent homes they so desperately need.
- ***Health***: Aside from the money the NHS spends on treating the effects of homelessness and bad

---

Many local education authorities make little or no provision for the needs of homeless children

---

housing, like chest infections and breathing problems, there are also costs for treating depression that can be worsened by poor housing conditions. The human cost of people forced to live in cold, damp and inadequate housing is too high a price to pay.
- ***Children***: Children's health and later their education can suffer from poor housing conditions. Many local education authorities make little or no provision for the needs of homeless children. It is difficult for a child to succeed at school if he or she has to change schools up to three times a year because their parents are in temporary accommodation.
- ***Welfare benefits***: Many people are caught in the benefits trap – rents are too high and housing benefit decreases sharply when people start earning. This can be a disincentive for taking jobs when they are offered. High rents mean that the housing benefit bill is high.

If you agree that homelessness costs, why not become involved in Shelter's work and help us to make a difference?

- The above information is from Shelter. See page 41 for address details.

© Shelter

Growing up homeless

The lives of homeless children

The impact of homelessness and poor housing on children's lives

This information examines the extent of homelessness, poor housing and poverty amongst children and considers the damaging effects on their education, health and development.

Unstable

It is important for children to enjoy the stability of a permanent home and the experience of homelessness is emotionally unsettling. Not surprisingly, health visitors have reported that the children of homeless parents experience above-average behavioural difficulties. Indicators of emotional problems such as bed wetting, temper tantrums, irritability and unhappiness can be directly linked to the number of housing problems a family is facing.

Education

Frequent moves and upheaval mean that homeless children are often not able to attend school regularly. Liaison between housing and education departments is patchy and many homeless children miss out on school altogether. In a study, it was found that over two-thirds of families in temporary accommodation with children of school age had to move their children between schools as a direct result of changes in temporary addresses. Many of these families encountered difficulties finding school places due to the instability of their housing situation. The introduction of school 'league tables' means that schools are often unwilling to spend time and resources on pupils with emotional and behavioural difficulties because it reflects badly on the performance of the school. Homeless children who do not change school may face long and expensive journeys to travel to their 'old' school from their new address. Research has shown that the vocabulary and development of homeless children is often behind that of others and these educational disadvantages can feed through into adult life, resulting in poor literacy skills and low self-esteem.

Friends

School is one of the range of networks which enable children to make friends and integrate into society. Homeless children are often outsiders in school and can be bullied and called names by other children. Children from temporary accommodation often do not interact with others in the same way as children from other households. The shortage of safe play areas in temporary housing means they may lack the social skills of other children such as the ability to play together, sharing space and toys. Many homeless families leave their local community to find temporary housing and so children are deprived of contact with neighbours, family and friends.

Health

Babies born in temporary accommodation tend to be small for their age and therefore more vulnerable to ill health. People who live in temporary housing are also likely to live in the most overcrowded conditions and councils are increasingly placing homeless families in private rented housing, which is generally of the poorest quality. So, on top of suffering the stress of losing their homes, homeless children also suffer the detrimental effects of living in poor housing. Children's poor health may be exacerbated by the obstacles homeless families face trying to register with a GP due to frequent moves, complex bureaucracy and the sometimes indifferent attitude of medical staff.

Poor housing

For every homeless child there are many more who live in homes that are damp, overcrowded or in poor condition, in neighbourhoods that are deprived and unsafe. A house only represents a home to a child if it is in good repair, safe, secure and of adequate size and design. Poor housing has devastating consequences on children's lives in terms of their physical and mental health. Over 1.5 million houses are classed as 'unfit' in England, of which over 90 per cent are lived in. The most common causes of unfitness are unsatisfactory facilities for the preparation and cooking of food, disrepair and dampness. Over three-

quarters of a million families with children live in poor housing defined as being either unfit, in substantial disrepair, or requiring essential modernisation.

Cold and damp

Cold and poorly ventilated homes can lead to dampness. Damp housing encourages the growth of mould and the spread of infectious disease. Children who live in damp and mouldy housing are more likely to suffer from respiratory problems, stomach upsets, aches and pains, fatigue and nervousness. Parental reports of wheezing, nocturnal coughing and school absence are significantly more common in damp and mouldy housing. Over 1.3 million children suffer from asthma causing more absence from school than any other condition. Living in deprived inner-city areas is linked to wheezing, asthma and respiratory problems in children.

Overcrowding

The legal definition of overcrowding has not changed since the 1930s – a living room or in some cases a kitchen can be considered by law a suitable place to sleep. Even against these unsatisfactory criteria it is estimated that 478,000 households live in statutorily overcrowded conditions. Thirteen per cent of families with two or more dependent children live in homes with less than three bedrooms. Apart from being stressful, overcrowding can blight the health and hinder the development of children in areas such as walking, co-ordination and speech skills. Overcrowding also puts children at increased risk of accidental death – more than one million children visit an Accident and Emergency Department each year following an accident in the home.

Children living in overcrowded housing and lacking appropriate study facilities find it hard to do homework and course projects out of school hours. A shortage of bedrooms causes sleep deprivation which interferes with a child's ability to concentrate during school hours. Ethnic minority families (which are on average larger) often bear the brunt of overcrowding in deprived inner-city areas. A GP in London's East End reported that it is not unusual for a family of ten to be cramped into a three-bedroom flat.

Children with disabilities

Children with disabilities are vulnerable to poor housing conditions. Average household incomes are lower in families with disabled children which limits their housing options. Four out of ten families with disabled children believe their housing is unsuitable for a disabled child: difficult stairs, lack of space, cold and damp are common problems.

© Shelter

The effects of homelessness on children

Living in temporary accommodation (bed and breakfast, hostels or short-term lets) for long periods, in poor, cramped conditions, makes a reasonable family life almost impossible, and can affect children's development in a number of ways:

- *Lack of a safe place to play.* Families in bed and breakfast and hostel accommodation have to carry on their lives in restricted surroundings. They often have to eat, sleep, sit, store clothes and cooking utensils in one or two rooms, leaving little space for toys or play. Young children are kept from crawling and exploring; older children have to be kept in check. It is estimated that children in multi-occupancy accommodation are twice as likely to have accidents and ten times more likely to die in fires than others.
- *Unsettled school life.* Disruption to education is a common experience. As their family is moved around, children have to cope with several changes of school, and may spend long periods with no schooling at all. In one study, 38% of the children were found to be out of school. If they try to stay at the same school, children and parents are likely to face long journeys each day. Lack of space at home means difficulties in doing homework.
- *Health and hygiene problems.* A common experience for families in temporary accommodation is unhygienic conditions and difficulty in maintaining good health and diet. Low birth weight in babies and respiratory tract infections in children are common. Homeless families often find it difficult to get on GPs' lists, and health visitors have difficulty in maintaining contact.
- *Emotional problems.* The security of children living in temporary accommodation is constantly undermined, without the stability of familiar surroundings. Many children in homeless families have already had experiences affecting their emotional and physical well-being. Some are refugees; some are escaping domestic violence; others have experienced eviction and multiple moves.
- *Loss of social and community support.* Homeless families are often housed far away from their original communities, with a resulting loss in ready support from friends and the wider family. Frequent moves make it difficult for children to make and keep friends at school. Families also have trouble in getting access to local facilities, such as day nurseries or family centres, and the social services have difficulty keeping in touch when families move from one area to another.

©Barnardo's

Youth homelessness

Information from NCH Action for Children

What does youth homelessness mean?

The term youth homelessness covers a number of different living situations. It includes young people living on the streets with no kind of shelter, but also those who have shelter, but nowhere they can call home – those sleeping in hostels or on friends' or relatives' floors.

The size of the problem

The scale of the problem is very difficult to assess. Official statistics are collected on the number of households who apply as homeless and the number who are accepted as being a priority for help. Young people are rarely accepted: they therefore tend not to apply so their housing need is underrepresented in these statistics.

The most recent estimates of youth homelessness have ranged from 33,000 (16-21-year-olds)[1] to 246,000[2] (16-25-year-olds). Because these figures are based on incomplete information and use different methodologies it is almost impossible to say which gives the most accurate insight into the scale of the problem.

What is clear is that the problem has worsened considerably over the last 10 years. Experts and organisations working in the field have attributed much of this rise to the withdrawal of benefit entitlement from the majority of 16- and 17-year-olds. Increases in divorce and remarriage and in youth unemployment have also contributed.

Causes of homelessness

In Great Britain high youth unemployment and low wages mean that many young people's dependence on their parents is prolonged. The number of young people between the ages of 20 and 24 still living at home with their parents has increased significantly since 1991 with over a half of men and a third of women of these ages still living with their parents[3].

Such prolonged dependence creates pressures on its own and is often compounded by poverty or poor housing conditions, so that tensions can increase to the point where a young person has little or no option but to leave.

Recent research[4] suggests that as many as 86% of young people who become homeless have been forced to leave home due to 'push factors' including violence, abuse, family breakdown and being thrown out. Some parents ask their children to leave because poverty means they have difficulty supporting them.

Recent research found that as many as 40% of young homeless women had experienced sexual abuse in childhood[5]. The proportion of young people – young men and young women – citing sexual or physical abuse as their reason for having left home is around 15%[6]. However, this may be an underrepresentation since problems of abuse and violence may not be reported initially, and are therefore disguised within categories such as household friction or parental problems[7].

Push factors such as family conflict may be particularly prevalent for some groups of young people. There is some evidence that same gender step-relationships can be more problematic than the average adolescent relationship[8]. The most stressful areas are divided loyalties and discipline, and the conflicts that arise can lead stepchildren to leave home. A survey of homeless young people in Scotland found that a quarter had a step-parent compared to four per cent of all young Scottish people[9].

Another group particularly at risk of homelessness due to family conflict are young people who are gay or lesbian. A significant proportion report being told to leave the family home when they reveal their sexuality[10]. Young lesbians and gay men are also vulnerable to homelessness as a result of harassment by landlords and neighbours[11].

Harassment is also a problem for black young people. Research[12] and practice evidence on young black people who become homeless shows that they tend to be better educated and are more likely to be employed. Unfortunately this is not the case for young black people generally and there must therefore be the possibility that we lack information about homelessness amongst those from black and ethnic minorities and that service provision may be failing to fully meet their needs.

Some young people are not in the position of having a family home. Surveys suggest that care leavers make up somewhere between a fifth and a half of the homeless population[13]. Much more needs to be done to improve the transition to

independent living for care leavers, nearly two-thirds of whom are discharged from care at 16. Whether or not they wish to be discharged from care, they may not be ready to live independently without significant amounts of support. Too often such support is not made available to them and the result is that the accommodation is lost and young people's one and only chance of avoiding youth homelessness is gone.

Those young people who leave home or care because they have to often do so in an unprepared and unplanned way with few, if any, resources or family support. As has been shown some care leavers have no support on offer. Young people in this position have difficulty finding and keeping alternative accommodation so are at very high risk of homelessness.

Whilst the factors listed above leave young people vulnerable to homelessness the most immediate cause of the problem is the difficulty they experience in gaining access to appropriate accommodation.

Young people suffer from disproportionately high levels of unemployment. The unemployment rate for those aged 16-24 is 14 per cent whilst the overall rate is relatively much lower, at 6 per cent[14]. Those who can find work often receive very low rates of pay. These factors mean that they are very unlikely to be in a position to buy their own home, but also make them an unattractive proposition for many private landlords. Many landlords are unwilling to let properties to those reliant on benefits for a variety of reasons, including the delays that often occur before housing benefit is paid. Twenty-two per cent of rented accommodation advertisements in *Loot* (2/12/95) for under £100 a week specify 'no DSS'.

Further, more recent changes in the way that housing benefit payments are assessed – such as the introduction of local reference rents, and the insistence on shared accom-modation for under-25s – appears to have made landlords even more reluctant to rent to young people reliant on housing benefit. Landlords believe that there will be a shortfall between the rent due

and the benefit allowed, and rightly question the ability of those on very low incomes to make up that shortfall.

When such difficulties are coupled with the commonly held perception of young people as 'difficult' it is easy to see that these young people are often last on the list of preferred tenants. Other barriers to acquiring private rented sector accommodation include requests for deposits and rent in advance.

Council and housing association properties are specifically designed for those on low incomes who may have trouble accessing private rented accommodation. However, demand for these properties far exceeds supply in most areas. Other problems are that council housing primarily caters for families, some councils will not lease to those under 21 and many do not lease to those under 18.

Legislative safety net

The homelessness legislation notionally provides a safety net for homeless people. However, in practice it is only those who are homeless and regarded as having a priority need who are provided with or given assistance with finding accommodation.

Young people are only regarded as a priority if they are considered vulnerable. Most local authorities do not regard young people (even those aged only 16 and 17) as vulnerable just because they are living on the streets. Even proof of risk of violence, abuse, or exploitation does not guarantee the granting of priority need status[15].

Some homeless young people may receive assistance from social services under the Children Act 1989. However, research shows that homelessness is not enough to entitle a 16- or 17-year-old to accommoda-

Youth homelessness – some facts

- The term youth homelessness includes young people living on the streets, and those sleeping in hostels or on friends' or relatives' floors.
- There is no reliable figure of the number of young people who are homeless. Estimates vary enormously – from 33,000 (16-21-year-olds) to 246,000 (16-25-year-olds).
- The number of young people between 20 and 24 still living at home with their parents has increased significantly since 1991 with over a half of men and a third of women of these ages still living with their parents.
- Recent Centrepoint research suggests that as many as 86% of young homeless people have been forced to leave home due to 'push factors' including violence, abuse, family breakdown and being thrown out.
- Research conducted by CHAR in 1992 found that as many as 40% of young homeless women had experienced sexual abuse in childhood.
- A survey of homeless young people in Scotland found that a quarter had a step-parent compared to four per cent of all young Scottish people.
- Another group particularly at risk of homelessness due to family conflict are young people who are gay or lesbian. A significant proportion report being told to leave the family home when they reveal their sexuality.
- Research conducted by Leeds University found that people from black and ethnic minorities were disproportionately represented amongst those most vulnerable to homelessness. The most common cause of homelessness was family breakdown.
- Some young people are not in the position of having a family home. Surveys suggest that care leavers make up somewhere between a fifth and a half of the homeless population.
- There is accommodation such as council and housing association properties specifically designed for those on low incomes. However, demand for these properties far exceeds supply in most areas and young people are not usually seen as a priority.

© Shelter

tion under the Act. Additional factors such as risk or experience of abuse seem to be required[16].

The safety net is barely more effective for young care leavers, with only a half of local authorities automatically regarding homeless care leavers as vulnerable[11]. There is no legal duty on a local authority to provide a care leaver with housing.

The government is seeking to improve provision for both these groups, but at present their chances of receiving adequate accommodation and support are low.

Many young people in the position of losing or having to leave their last permanent address therefore find themselves with literally nowhere to go. Others are lucky enough to have friends or extended family who can provide them with a floor or a sofa to sleep on, but such arrangements are only workable in the short term.

The consequences of youth homelessness

Being homeless has a devastating impact on young people's ability to develop and reach their full potential.

Although unemployment contributes to homelessness the circle is a vicious one. Without a home it becomes even more difficult to get a job. Up to 80 per cent of young homeless people are unemployed[17].

Unsurprisingly, health problems are highly prevalent amongst young homeless people with over 70 per cent reporting poor health, a fact not helped by their difficulty in accessing health services. Young homeless people are twice as likely to suffer from mental health problems[18]. Research also shows high rates of alcohol and drug misuse[19].

Strong links have also been found between offending and homelessness[20]. The crimes involved tend to be antisocial (often alcohol-related) or self-preservatory – committed in order to obtain money or food, thus begging and prostitution are common. Those young people with an alcohol or drug problem have an increased risk of being drawn into crime or prostitution.

Conclusion

Youth homelessness makes us all poorer, as well as being personally devastating for those young people affected. Society not only wastes valuable resources in terms of the unused talents and energies of those young people but often pays a high cost in terms of the need to provide intensive and expensive resettlement or restraint.

References
1 London Research Centre, *Estimates of young single homelessness – A report to NCH Action for Children*, 1996.
2 Evans, A., *We Don't Choose to Be Homeless – The Findings of the Inquiry into Preventing Youth Homelessness*, CHAR 1996.
3 Holman, A., Household formation by Young Men and Young Women, in *Housing in England 1994/5*, Social Survey Division of the Office of National Statistics on behalf of the Department of the Environment, HMSO, 1996.
4 Nassor, I.A.A. and Simms, A., *The New Picture of Homelessness in Britain*, Youth Affairs Briefing, Centrepoint, London, 1996.
5 Centrepoint Annual Statistics.
6 Hendessi, M., *Four in Ten*, CHAR, 1992.
7 Scottish Association of Citizen's Advice Bureaux.
8 Schlösser, A. and De'Ath, E., *Keeping in Touch: Looked after children and their step-families*, Fact File 2, National Stepfamily Association, London, 1994.
9 Jones, G., *Leaving Home*, Open University Press, 1995.
10 London Gay Teenager Group.
11 Stonewall submission to CHAR Housing Inquiry 1996.
12 Davies, J., Lyle, S., et al., *Discounted Voices – Homelessness amongst young black and minority ethnic people in England*, University of Leeds, 1996.
13 e.g. *Carefree and Homeless; Why so many careleavers are homeless and will the Children Act make a difference?*, Young Homelessness Group, 1991. Anderson, I., Kemp, P., and Quilgars, D., *Single Homeless People*, Department of the Environment, HMSO, 1993. Centrepoint Annual Statistics.
14 Labour Force Survey, Summer 1996.
15 Kay, H., *Conflicting Priorities: Homeless 16- and 17-year-olds: A changing agenda for housing authorities?*, CHAR, Chartered Institute of Housing, 1994.
16 McCluskey, J., *Acting in Isolation – An evaluation of the effectiveness of the Children Act for young homeless people*, CHAR, 1994.
17 Anderson, I., Kemp, P., and Quilgars, D., *Single Homeless People*, Department of the Environment, 1993.
18 *Off to a Bad Start*, The Mental Health Foundation, 1996.
19 Flemen, K., *Smoke and Whispers*, Turning Point Hungerford Project, 1995.
20 Association of Chief Officers of Probation, 1993 study quoted in Nacro Occasional Paper 1993.

© NCH Action for Children

Factors precipitating homelessness

In March 1999, 24 per cent of thsoe accepted for assistance cited relationship breakdown as the cause of their housing crisis.

Source: Department of the Environment Transport and the Regions Information Bulletin, June 1999.

Why are so many young people homeless?

Unemployment and pay

Young people can be trapped in a cycle of homelessness and unemployment. Without work it is difficult to find a place to live but it is almost impossible to get a job without a permanent address. In spring 1996, the unemployment rate for 16- to 24-year-olds was around 15% – roughly twice the national average (*Labour Force Survey Quarterly Bulletin*, HMSO, 1996). Many of those in work were in part-time or insecure jobs with low incomes. This lack of certainty can make it difficult to get a home.

Even young people in full-time employment may not be able to afford housing. Most young people are on low wages, earning on average between £126.70 and £242.60 per week (dependent upon age and gender) compared to the average for all ages which is £348.50 (*New Earnings Survey*, 1996). In April 1995, the average rent for a one-bedroom home in London was £153.59 which is therefore beyond the reach of many young working people (*Private Sector Rents Bulletin*, London Research Centre, No. 10). The cost of good housing means that young people are forced into cheaper options such as renting a room in a house that has been divided into small flats, studio flats and bedsits. These are known as Houses in Multiple Occupation (HMOs). They can carry increased fire risks and are generally of poor quality.

Benefits

Since 1988 most unemployed 16 and 17-year-olds have not been automatically entitled to income support unless they are undertaking Youth Training. However, there are not enough Youth Training places for all of them. If living independently, 16- and 17-year-olds may claim a discretionary hardship payment but these are difficult to obtain and are only awarded for a few weeks at a time.

The number of 16- and 17-year-olds who successfully made new claims for severe hardship payments in a given month has risen from 1,669 in May 1990 to 10,376 in April 1996 (Youthaid, 1996). Despite this increase, 42% of the young people arriving at Centrepoint hostels in 1995 had no income whatsoever. (*Annual Statistics*, Centrepoint, 1995).

From October 1996, the Job Seekers Allowance (JSA) replaced income support and unemployment benefit for those who have to register for work. Income support was previously paid to young people between 18- and 25-years of age at a reduced rate although those claiming unemployment benefit received the full rate. The JSA is paid at a reduced rate for all 18 to 25 year olds who are eligible. This means that some young people who were claiming unemployment benefit will suffer a cut in benefits. However, they face the same costs of living, rent, food, travel, fuel bills and so on as older people.

Housing benefit is only paid in full up to a local reference rent set by Rent Officers. The local reference rent for private rented homes is based on the size and location of the dwelling. Where the rent for a property is above the local reference rent, housing benefit will only cover half the difference between the local reference and actual rent. The local reference rent for single people under the age of 25 is based on shared not self-contained accommodation. For some young people shared accommodation is not a suitable option. If a young person on housing benefit takes up self-contained accommodation after October 1996, they will have to pay the remaining from their own income or face eviction.

The poverty trap

When a person receiving benefits starts work, the combined effect of benefit withdrawal, national insurance and income tax mean that real income is reduced at almost the same rate as earnings increase. Unless the earnings are substantially above the value of the benefits, people may end up worse off by working, once costs such as travel and clothing are taken into account.

Leaving care and nowhere to go

Care leavers become independent much younger than most other young people, often with little or no support from family and friends. They do not enjoy the option of occasionally returning 'home' to be looked after. Young care leavers can be expected to immediately cope on their own and may not have had the opportunity to learn life skills such as budgeting and housekeeping.

Under the Children Act 1989, social service departments have duties and powers to provide accommodation and support to care leavers. However, a shortage of funding and the discretionary status of many of the provisions mean the quality of service is inconsistent. For example, around a quarter (23%) of young people leaving care say they had no support from any source (*Prepared for Living: Leaving Care Research Project*, University of Leeds, 1992).

With a lack of support young care leavers are more likely to become homeless. A DoE study in 1991 found that over half the 16- and 17-year olds and 39 per cent of 18- to 24-year-olds living in temporary accommodation had lived in care, hospital or other type of institution at some point previously. (*Single Homeless People* HMSO, 1993).

Forced to leave home

Recent research by Centrepoint with 7,500 homeless young people in seven different locations across the country found that 86 per cent had been forced to leave home rather than choosing to leave (*The New Picture of Youth Homelessness*, Centrepoint, 1996). Reasons included:

- family arguments
- relationship breakdown
- overcrowding
- physical and sexual violence.

In 1991, a study by CHAR found that four in ten homeless young women had suffered sexual abuse prior to becoming homeless (*Four in Ten*, CHAR, 1992).

The Government has argued that young homeless people should return to their families rather than rely on social security. This is in spite of the evidence that the majority do not have homes to go back to.

Asylum seekers

In 1995, the Refugee Council housed 2,591 asylum seekers and refugees and 48 per cent of these were between 17 and 25 years of age. During 1996 the Government passed the Asylum and Immigration Act 1996 which curtails the housing and social security rights of asylum seekers who do not apply at the port of entry and those who are appealing against the refusal of their application. This will leave many young people who have already suffered traumatic experiences before coming to this country destitute and reliant on charitable donations and community provision.

Discrimination

Within society young people are often stereotyped as feckless and irresponsible. This can affect their ability to find somewhere to live. Minority groups face added discrimination. In 1989, the Commission for Racial Equality found that one in five accommodation agencies were consistently discriminating against black clients. The Commission also found that a local authority had housed white homeless families far quicker than black families with the same housing needs. Many lesbians and gay men suffer harassment and abuse due to their sexuality and have to leave their homes. Almost half of those applying to Stonewall, a London housing association for young lesbians and gay men, said that harassment by landlords, neighbours and others was a factor in their homelessness (*The Inquiry into Preventing Youth Homelessness*, CHAR, 1996). Young disabled people also face severe accommodation problems because of the lack of adequate housing. In April 1995, there were only 147,761 disabled access homes in England.

- The above information is an extract from *Young People and Homelessness*, produced by Shelter. See page 41 for address details.

© *Shelter*

Shortage of rural homes 'leaves young on streets'

Youth homelessness is growing in rural areas because of a 'disgraceful' shortage of low-cost housing, says a report by the Countryside Agency and Centrepoint, the young people's charity.

The common perception is that youth homelessness is confined to London and major cities. But the report shows that those in rural areas facing the breakdown of their homes have 'little hope' of help locally.

People aged 16-25 cannot afford private rents because of competition from second-home owners and tourists, planning rules and Government limits on housing benefit, says the three-year study released yesterday. It says that the lack of emergency accommodation for the young homeless, of the kind Centrepoint provides in towns and cities, and the acute shortage of council or housing association homes, pushes young people into towns and cities where they are disorientated and susceptible to drugs, violence and prostitution.

By Charles Clover, Environment Editor

Centrepoint's research found young people sleeping in tents, on playing fields, in cars and vans and under motorway bridges. Many are 'sofa surfing' on floors and couches of friends. Jo Gunner, author of the study, said there was an 'absolute lack' of affordable housing. She said: 'There is a complete lack of awareness that homelessness exists at all in rural areas.'

Victor Adebowale, chief executive of Centrepoint, said: 'Our

An estimated 200,000 young people are thought to be homeless nationally, with 14 per cent officially recorded as being in rural areas

work in Devon and across the country highlights the problems of poverty, low wages and the lack of affordable housing. Time and again we find that help, advice and housing simply isn't there when young people need it most, for example when family support breaks down and they are thrown out of home.'

Ewen Cameron, chairman of the Countryside Agency, said the right to buy council houses had been 'disastrous' for rural areas, removing 91,000 council homes from the rental market. An estimated 200,000 young people are thought to be homeless nationally, with 14 per cent officially recorded as being in rural areas.

Centrepoint and the agency say there were many hidden homeless people in rural areas not included in the official statistics. The report recommends emergency housing for the young in all districts and an end to benefit restrictions.

© *Telegraph Group Limited, London 2000*

The hidden homeless

Key points from a study of black and minority ethnic homelessness in London

- Black and minority ethnic groups accounted for 49% of hidden homeless households. Additionally 9% were Irish.
- There were significantly more males (61.2%) than females (37.4%). Nearly half (44.9%) were under 26 years of age. The majority (75.2%) were unemployed including 7.6% who had no income. Some 98% of all respondents had income below £200 per week and just over half had income of less than £50 per week. The majority were single (83%) and just under 10% included a member of the household who was either pregnant or had children.
- A breakdown in relationships (39.9%), particularly in the family, was the most common cause of homelessness. Addiction to alcohol or drugs was the most common contributory factor which was cited by 15.5% of respondents.
- The majority of users of day centres and outreach teams are white (77%) including 20.6% who are Irish. Black groups did however feature more highly amongst day centres that were targeted at minority ethnic groups, young people or women.
- With few exceptions the black groups were the predominant respondents from hostels (57.7%), independent housing advice centres (61%) and local authority advice centres (50%).
- The black (57.1%) and other (55.5%) groups had a higher proportion of respondents under 26 years of age, compared to the Asian (37.3%) and white (34.7%) groups.
- Generally men are more likely to be homeless than women however, black (46.3%) and Asian women (43.1%) are more likely to be homeless than white women (28.7%).
- Single people formed the majority of all ethnic groups. The Asian groups formed the lowest proportion of single-person households with 75.5%.
- All black and minority ethnic groups were more likely to be working or studying than the white group.
- The Asian groups had significantly less contact with homelessness agencies which makes the extent of homelessness for Asian communities difficult to measure. Further research is required to gain a better understanding of homelessness for, and the services used by, the Asian communities.
- The type of temporary accommodation available to homeless people militates against the needs of independent people over 25 years of age. This can lead to older people being without appropriate accommodation for longer periods of time.
- Those providing accommodation need to consider access routes to independent accommodation. It may be appropriate to give some priority to people with parental responsibility (but not custody) of a child.
- The propensity for men to become homeless, the ethnic composition of homeless households and the age structures need to be considered when determining targets for the allocation of accommodation provided by social registered landlords and voluntary housing projects.
- It will be difficult to reduce homelessness and sustain economic and social stability without a reduction in rent levels and increased rent control. This needs to be considered alongside a workable strategy to increase employment prospects and wage levels particularly for young black males.

• The above information is an extract from *The Hidden Crisis*, a book produced by Frontline. See page 41 for address details.   © *Frontline*

Single homeless people

Information from Shelter

Health problems

Single homeless people make up the vast majority of rough sleepers and those who stay in night-shelters and short-term hostels. Few people can doubt that sleeping rough is bad for people's health. The physical problems associated with sleeping rough include respiratory problems, foot problems, skin complaints, muscle and joint problems, stomach and digestive disorders, accidents and high rates of premature death.

The average age of death of someone who sleeps rough is 42 years, compared to the national average of 74 for men and 79 for women. This is partly because rough sleepers are four times as likely to die of unnatural causes than the general population. However the average age of death from natural causes for rough sleepers is only 46 years. Single homeless people experience levels of tuberculosis (TB) that are twenty-five times the level of the general population.

Research has shown that compared to the general population people who sleep rough are:

- three times more likely to suffer from chronic chest or breathing problems
- twice as likely to experience muscle and joint problems
- twice as likely to have digestive problems
- three times more likely to experience frequent headaches.

Why do single homeless people suffer from poor health?

People sleeping rough experience the effects of severe weather and poor nutrition, and have limited access to hygiene facilities. A dose of flu which a housed person would shake off within days can be a serious illness for someone with nowhere to live.

Health is often not a priority for homeless people. Keeping warm and finding something to eat comes first. Homeless people suffer from the lack of a balanced diet due to a lack of money and because an irregular lifestyle makes it difficult to plan meals ahead.

Alcohol and drug misuse affects some homeless people but by no means the majority.

Alcohol misuse affects between a third and a half of rough sleepers which is about 1.5 times the rate in the general population. Alcohol is linked to epilepsy, liver damage, muscle wastage, paralysis and general deterioration in physical health. One study found that three per cent of people in hostels, seven per cent of people in day centres and nine per cent of people at soup runs had problems relating to non-prescription drugs.

Hostels and night-shelters are often overcrowded and poorly ventilated which creates the ideal conditions for the transmission of diseases. Sleeping on the street or staying in hostels can be very dangerous. Homeless people are one hundred and fifty times more likely to be fatally assaulted than the general population.

Homelessness compounds the health problems of those who already suffer from ill health. Some people may have lost their homes and jobs as a result of ill health, drink dependency or HIV status. Their subsequent chaotic lifestyle on the street and in hostels will make them even more vulnerable to poor health.

- The above information is an extract from *Homelessness and Health* produced by Shelter. See page 41 for address details. © *Shelter*

Myths about homeless people

- *Homeless people jump the council housing queue.* In 1995/96, more than half of council tenancies went to people on the waiting list. Only 25% of tenancies went to homeless families. Most authorities' waiting lists gave priority to the length of time on the list, and a points system for poor housing and health conditions.
- *Young women get pregnant in order to get their own home.* There is no evidence for this. One study of single mothers found that seeking to obtain accommodation played a negligible role in the decision to have a child. Another found that it was rare for unmarried teenage mothers, or expectant mothers, to apply for rehousing as homeless.
- *Black people get housed more quickly.* In fact, minority ethnic groups suffer disproportionately from homelessness. In London during 1996, 51 per cent of households accepted as homeless were from an ethnic minority, whereas minority ethnic groups make up just 18% of London's population. They have more difficulty in obtaining accommodation as a result of discrimination, low income and high unemployment, and they are likely to wait longer in temporary accommodation before being rehoused.
- *If homeless people get a job, they could afford a home.* About half of families registering as homeless have one member in employment, but renting privately is expensive, and most landlords require deposits. In 1993 it was estimated that a single mother with one child in London would have to earn twice the national average wage to cover the average rent in the private sector.
- *Homelessness doesn't last long.* In London, many families are spending over two years in temporary accommodation, during which time they will have several changes of address, often at short notice. Larger families may have to wait four years or more for a permanent home.

© *Barnardo's*

Mental health and homelessness

Extent of mental health problems among single homeless people

It is difficult to obtain accurate data on the mental health of homeless people because data from the studies are dependent on the definition or approach used by researchers. Some studies have suggested that as many as 50 per cent of the total homeless population may have some form of mental health problems.

According to Bines (1994) the proportion of homeless single people experiencing mental health problems is 28 per cent of people in hostels and bed and breakfast hotels (B&B), 36 per cent of day centre users and 40 per cent of soup run users, compared to 5 per cent of the general population.

A Shelter study (1996) found that 10 per cent of homeless people attending an Accident and Emergency Department (A&E) in a London hospital had mental health problems. This compared with only 3 per cent of the housed attenders. Mental illness was the second reason, after accidents and injuries, for homeless people attending A&E.

Women

A study by Marshall and Reed (1992) among residents of two direct access hostels which cater specifically for homeless women, found that 64 per cent of women met the criteria for schizophrenia and a further 26 per cent suffered from other psychiatric disorders.

Young people

The occurrence of mental health problems in the general population increases with age. Older people are more likely to suffer mental health problems. However, among single homeless people, those aged between 25 and 59 were most likely to suffer mental health problems (Bines, 1994). Bines reported that depression was relatively high among young

homeless people compared with the general population. A recent study estimates that about two-thirds of young homeless people were suffering mental health problems (Craig et al, 1996).

Rough sleepers

Rough sleepers are often those most adversely affected by mental health problems. A survey carried out by the Office of Population Censuses and Surveys (Gil, B et al, 1996) found that nearly 60 per cent of rough sleepers using day centres have some form of mental health problems. A Shelter study (1996) found that 51 per cent of homeless men and 34 per cent of women attending an A&E in London suffering psychotic illness were of 'no fixed abode'.

All these studies suggest that this is a vulnerable group living in conditions that make it very difficult, if not impossible, to gain access to psychiatric and social services. This results in further deterioration of their mental health.

Black and minority ethnic people

Black and ethnic minority people are disproportionately represented both in the homeless population and on admission to psychiatric institutions. Forty-nine per cent of those accepted as homeless in London are from ethnic minority groups. People from ethnic minorities are three times as likely to be admitted to a psychiatric institution than the general population (CHAR, 1993).

References
Bines, W (1994) *The Health of single homeless people*. Centre for Housing Policy, York University.
CHAR (1993) *Homing in on health: A Resource pack on health and homelessness*.
Craig, TKJ (1996) *Off to a bad start*. Mental Health Foundation.
Gil, B et al (1996) *The prevalence of psychiatric morbidity among homeless adults*. Office of Population Censuses & Survey.
Marshall, E & Reed, J (1992) Psychiatric morbidity in homeless women. *British Journal of Psychiatry*.
Shelter (1996) *Go home and rest: The use of an accident and emergency department by homeless people*.

• The above information is an extract from *Homelessness and Health* produced by Shelter. See page 41 for address details.

© *Shelter*

House the homeless and cut crime

Information from the National Association for the Care and Resettlement of Offenders (Nacro)

Homelessness creates crime, according to a new report from Nacro released today (13 December 1999). The report, *Going Straight Home*, argues that providing stable housing for ex-offenders and other vulnerable people is an essential ingredient in promoting safer communities.

Figures suggest that homeless ex-prisoners are twice as likely to commit another crime as those who have a home to go to. Homelessness and unstable living conditions can be a key risk factor that makes it more likely that someone will offend. Nacro research on imprisoned young offenders, published last November, found that 60% of those questioned had experienced unstable living conditions. The government's Social Exclusion Unit has found that around half of rough sleepers have been in a prison or remand centre at some time.

Paul Cavadino, Nacro's Director of Policy and co-author of the report, said, 'Most homeless people are law abiding. However, vulnerable people without a home are more likely to drift into crime, and prisoners are more likely to reoffend if they have no home to go to on release. If we are serious about stopping people committing crime, we must be serious about tackling homelessness.'

Tim Bell, Nacro's Director of Housing and co-author of the report, said, 'Access to adequate housing, and the crucial stability this provides, is often key to leading a law-abiding life, not an optional extra or reward for good behaviour. This means that the housing of offenders should always be a question of "how" and "where" rather than "if". There is little sense in evicting offenders, or stopping them from getting housing in the first place, if all we do is displace the problem of homelessness and crime elsewhere.'

'Excluding offenders from housing leads to crime,' the new Nacro report says

Key facts

- A 1993 survey of users of hostels, bed and breakfast, day centres and soup runs found that the majority had been in custody in the last five years.
- A 1998 Nacro survey of young offenders found that 60% of those questioned had experienced unstable living conditions.
- A Social Exclusion Unit report in 1998 found that around half of rough sleepers had been in prison or a remand centre at some time.
- A Home Office study of released prisoners found that less than one-third of prisoners who had homes to go to were reconvicted, compared with 69% of homeless prisoners.

Ex-offenders

Significant numbers of ex-offenders face homelessness. Statistics have shown a higher incidence of people without settled accommodation amongst those who receive both custodial and non-custodial sentences. There is also evidence from hostels showing significant proportions of ex-offenders amongst applicants and residents.

Prisoners often lose their accommodation, either because of inability to pay rent whilst inside or because of family break-up and associated loss of home. Having nowhere to go on release is a common problem. Many ex-offenders are unemployed or on low incomes which also contributes to difficulties in finding somewhere to stay. Housing is a key component in resettlement of prisoners and settled accommodation is often a vital component in avoiding a return to crime.

Offenders with mental health problems face particular difficulties in finding and keeping accommodation. Research shows that some mentally vulnerable and homeless people get trapped in a 'revolving door'—a cyclical pattern of recurring homelessness, hospital admissions, arrests and possible imprisonment.

In London, there are a number of specialist hostels and housing projects for ex-offenders, and many other hostels have bedspaces reserved for ex-offenders and probation referrals. None the less, there are relatively few projects that will accept serious offenders. In particular, sex offenders and people convicted of arson find obtaining hostel or other accommodation extremely difficult.

• The above information is an extract from Homeless Pages, a web site dedicated to the issues of homelessness. It can be found at www.homelesspages.org.uk Homeless Pages contains details of the relatively small amount of research and other resources on ex-offenders, homelessness and housing issues.

- A Prisons Inspectorate survey in 1997 found that around 25% of young prisoners on reception were homeless or had experienced insecure accommodation.

Key proposals

- 'Blanket bans' on offenders should not be used by housing providers.

- There should be more investment in affordable rented housing.
- Prisons should help inmates make arrangements to keep existing homes and make systematic plans for housing on release.
- Housing benefit restrictions which have reduced benefit below the real level of rent should be reversed.

- Evictions should be followed through to ensure that contact is maintained and that offending behaviour is not simply displaced to another area.

- The above information is from Nacro. See page 41 for address details.

© Nacro

Who sleeps rough?

Backgrounds and contributory factors

How many?

- Over the course of a year, at least 2,400 people spend some time sleeping rough in London. 1,800 are new arrivals. Many are diverted quickly into hostels or other accommodation, while others drift in and out of rough sleeping for longer periods, and a hard core is out every night for months. The total on any given night (counted by the voluntary sector, in the small hours) averages about 400.
- These numbers have fallen dramatically from 2,000 a night sleeping rough in central London in the early 1990s, following sustained efforts by the voluntary sector, with considerable financial support from government, mainly through the Rough Sleepers Initiative (RSI).
- Data outside London are less robust. It is estimated that in England perhaps 2,000 sleep rough each night which probably means 10,000 drift in and out of rough sleeping over the course of a year. Single night counts in 1996 showed that the largest concentrations of rough sleepers reported are in Birmingham, Brighton, Cambridge, Manchester, Oxford and Bristol which recorded the highest number of 84.
- Many people find these numbers surprisingly low: the counts undoubtedly miss some people who sleep out in more inaccessible places. Public

impressions of the extent of rough sleeping are also influenced by the number of people who are seen begging, drinking, or apparently living on the streets during the day. Many people in this category do have somewhere to stay, if only temporarily, and some have flats, but come to the streets for company or begging opportunities. Some are former rough sleepers. One review of street drinker surveys found that only 20 per cent were sleeping rough, with half to two-thirds living in hostels or bed and breakfast hotels.

Who and from where?

We know less than we should about the backgrounds of people who sleep rough. Rough sleepers are by definition hard to keep track of, and some refuse to co-operate with surveys. Much of the research and survey work that has been done is small scale, and much relates to homeless people in general, of whom rough sleepers are only a small minority. (In the homelessness legislation a person is 'homeless' if he or she has no right to occupy property, for example, as an owner or tenant. Many people in temporary accommodation such as hostels, or

Highest concentrations of rough sleepers in England

Westminster	234		Croydon	25
Camden	66		Cambridge	21
Oxford	52		Waltham Forest	20
Lambeth	46		Slough	20
Manchester	44		Gloucester	20
Birmingham	43		Brent	19
Brighton and Hove	43		Exeter	19
City of London	36		Bournemouth	18
Bristol	32		York	18
Nottingham City	31		Ealing	18
Stoke on Trent	31		Leeds	17
Liverpool	30		Penwith	17
Kensington and Chelsea	28		Richmond upon Thames	16
Southwark	26		Hammersmith and Fulham	16
Chester	26		Watford	15

Total 1,047

Source: Department for the Environment Transport and the Regions (DETR)

those sharing with family or friends, are therefore technically homeless, but not sleeping rough.)

The information we do have tells us that:

- there are now very few rough sleepers aged under 18;
- around 25 per cent are between 18 and 25;
- six per cent are over 60; and
- around 90 per cent are male.

Proportions of rough sleepers from ethnic minorities are typically five per cent or less. But voluntary organisations report that there are disproportionately high numbers of people from ethnic minorities amongst the single homeless population who live in hostels.

Geographical origin of those coming to London appears to have changed over the last decade: Centrepoint report that an increasing proportion (now 60 per cent) of young homeless in the West End come from London itself, concentrated in a few boroughs. They now see more people from the London Boroughs of Lambeth, Lewisham and Southwark than from all of Scotland and Ireland put together.

Family background

The single most common reason given for the first episode of rough sleeping is relationship breakdown, either with parents or partner:

- research by Centrepoint with homeless young people across the country found that 86 per cent had been forced to leave home rather than choosing to;
- a study of young homeless people in Staffordshire found that those who had grown up with the same parents (or step-parents) for years, were most likely to become homeless because of conflicts about their own behaviour (e.g. exclusion from school, contributing to household expenses, involvement in crime/drugs, or arguments about friends). Those from families where parents had separated were most likely to become homeless because of conflicts with their parent or parent's new partner;
- a survey in Scotland found that a quarter of young homeless people

had a step-parent compared with the four per cent average for Scotland as a whole; and

- homelessness agencies report that physical or sexual abuse lies behind a significant minority of family conflicts, and one study found that 40 per cent of young women who become homeless had experienced sexual abuse in childhood or adolescence.

Older homeless people also identify family crises as key with the main factor being widowhood and marital breakdown, as well as eviction, redundancy and mental illness. One study showed that:

- over half the elderly homeless questioned had experienced broken or disturbed homes in their own childhood;
- they were about eight times more likely than average for their age group never to have married, and five times more likely to be divorced; and
- of those who had children, over half had had no contact with them for more than five years.

Institutional background

A disproportionate number of rough sleepers have experience of some kind of institutional life.

Local authority care

Between a quarter and a third of rough sleepers have been looked after by local authorities as children. Some young people run away from care repeatedly before they are officially discharged: one survey of young homeless people in London found that half had run away from a previous care arrangement, with a third having done so on more than nine occasions. Early discharge is also common: surveys have found that 60 per cent of those in care at the age of 16 are no longer being looked after by the age of 18. By comparison,

---

The single most common reason given for the first episode of rough sleeping is relationship breakdown, either with parents or partner

---

the average age of leaving home for the general population is 22.

Unlike other young people leaving home, many care leavers lack any sort of ongoing parental support which can act as a back-up when a first attempt at independent living goes wrong. Under the homelessness legislation a local authority has a duty to accommodate someone who is unintentionally homeless and has a priority need. Most care leavers would have a priority need because of their vulnerability. However, because the assessment rests with each local authority, different practice has evolved in different areas, and the homelessness safety net works less well in some places than others.

Prison

Around half of rough sleepers have been in prison or a remand centre at some time. Those who have been in prison typically experience serious problems obtaining both housing and jobs, frequently exacerbated by the problems of relationship breakdown, drugs etc. Research in prisons showed that 40 per cent of prisoners were homeless on release. Another study found that less than half of prisoners were able to return to the address at which they had lived before they entered custody. Some find that tenancies have lapsed or rent arrears built up while they were in prison and that as a result they are deemed to have made themselves intentionally homeless, and will not be rehoused.

Other rough sleepers only come into contact with the criminal justice system once they have started sleeping rough. One study found that 45 per cent of arrests of people with no fixed abode in one London borough were for drunk and disorderly or begging offences.

The armed forces

Repeated studies have found that between a quarter and one-fifth of rough sleepers have been in the Services at some stage. But many had left the Services some years ago – a few were ex-national Servicemen – before the introduction of comprehensive resettlement advice, and some had been in civilian employment since leaving. Nevertheless, in one survey two-fifths of homeless ex-Servicemen said they had never settled after being discharged.

Mental and physical health, drugs and alcohol

Some 30-50 per cent of rough sleepers suffer from mental health problems. The great majority (88 per cent) of those with mental health problems became ill before they became homeless.

Research does not support the widespread belief that the closure of long-term psychiatric hospitals has resulted in former patients sleeping rough: a number of studies have found that very few rough sleepers who are seriously mentally ill have ever been in long-stay hospitals. However, it has been found that less than a third of single homeless people with mental health problems were receiving treatment.

As many as 50 per cent of rough sleepers have a serious alcohol problem and some 20 per cent misuse drugs. Drug problems are more common amongst younger rough sleepers. Research carried out in 1996 found that 39 per cent of people sleeping rough under 26 had a drugs problem. The 1997 London Street Monitor estimated that about a third of rough sleepers in central London had multiple needs (most commonly substance abuse combined with mental health problems).

Education

Rough sleepers are disproportionately likely to have missed school. One Centrepoint study found that over three-quarters of homeless teenagers were either long-term non-attenders or had been excluded from school. A study by the *Big Issue in the North* found that ten per cent of their vendors stopped going to school when they were 13 or younger, and 47 per cent at 15 or younger. Another study found that only 38 per cent of rough sleepers have any educational qualifications (compared with 66 per cent of the general population).

The impact of housing and benefits policies

Generally, single people will only get assistance under the homelessness

legislation if they are unintentionally homeless and in priority need. If so, they can expect to have accommodation found or provided for them for two years and will get priority in the allocation of long-term housing through the waiting list. Most local authorities will put other single people on the waiting list, although the chances of being offered accommodation vary widely. In areas of high demand (for example, most of London), there is little prospect of a single person obtaining social housing unless they have special needs, and the alternative is the private rented sector. In some areas outside London where demand is low local authority accommodation is easier to come by for single people. Preference is usually given to those who already have a connection with the area.

Researchers generally agree that a number of changes in social security policy (e.g. the abolition of grants for rent deposits and furniture, and of board and lodging payments) in the late 1980s were closely associated with a squeeze on the ability of single people on low incomes to gain access to suitable housing. Many of the people we have consulted have cited past benefit changes as one of the key reasons for the increase in rough sleeping in the late 1980s. However, all these benefit changes affected far more people than ended up on the

streets. One of the common aims of these policies has been to discourage young people from leaving home to set up on their own.

More recently concern has been expressed about the possible effect on rough sleepers of the housing benefit single room rent restriction and the Department of Social Security is looking at this aspect in evaluating the effect of the policy. As foreshadowed in the Welfare Reform Green Paper the Government is reviewing the relationship between housing policy and housing benefit. The Ministerial Task Force on the Utting Report is also looking at the particular problems faced by care leavers who claim benefits.

The rapid rise in numbers of people sleeping rough in the early 1990s was concentrated in London, and exacerbated by the difficulty of co-ordinating action across boroughs and other agency boundaries. In response to this the last Government developed the Rough Sleepers Initiative run by the Department of the Environment, Transport and the Regions, which cut the numbers of people sleeping rough in central London substantially.

Rough sleepers

Information from the National Housing Federation

The health of rough sleepers is very poor

- People sleeping rough have an incidence of a range of physical health problems two to three times higher than that of the general population.
- A study by the coroner's court found that death by unnatural causes was for rough sleepers four times more common than average and that suicide was thirty times more likely.
- The mortality rate for a rough sleeper is between 3.8 and 5.6 times that of the general population.
- The estimated cost to the NHS of treating illnesses arising from homelessness and bad housing is £2.4 billion a year. Homeless families have an increased rate of unplanned admission to hospital 1.55 times that of the general population.
- Pregnant homeless women have three times the rate of antenatal complications and twice the unplanned admission rate of all pregnant women.
- Chronic chest or breathing problems are twice as high among people in hostels and B&Bs.
- Digestive problems are eight times as high among people in hostels and B&Bs.

Who sleeps rough?

- Over the year at least 2,400 people spend some time sleeping rough in London.
- 1,800 are new arrivals
- The total on any given night in London (counted by the voluntary sector, in the small hours) averages around 400.
- Single night counts in 1996 showed that the largest concentrations of rough sleepers outside London are: Birmingham, Brighton, Cambridge, Manchester, Oxford and Bristol which had the highest figure of 84.
- One view of street drinkers found that only 20 per cent were sleeping rough, with half to two-thirds living in hostels or bed and breakfast accommodation.

The Government's Social Exclusion report on Rough Sleeping showed that:

- There are very few rough sleepers aged under 18.
- Around 25 per cent are between 18 and 25.
- Six per cent are over 60.
- 90 per cent are male.
- Reports in prisons show that 40 per cent of prisoners were homeless on release.
- 30-50 per cent of rough sleepers suffer from mental health problems. The great majority (88 per cent) of those with mental health problems became ill before they became homeless.
- A third of rough sleepers have been in care.
- Half have been in prison or on remand at some time.
- 50 per cent of rough sleepers have a serious alcohol problem.
- 20 per cent misused drugs.
- 1996 research showed that 39 per cent of people sleeping rough under the age of 26 had a drugs problem.
- A centrepoint study found that 75 per cent of homeless teenagers were either long-term non-attenders or had been excluded from school.
- 38 per cent of rough sleepers have any educational qualifications (compared with 66 per cent of the general population).

© National Housing Federation
January, 2000

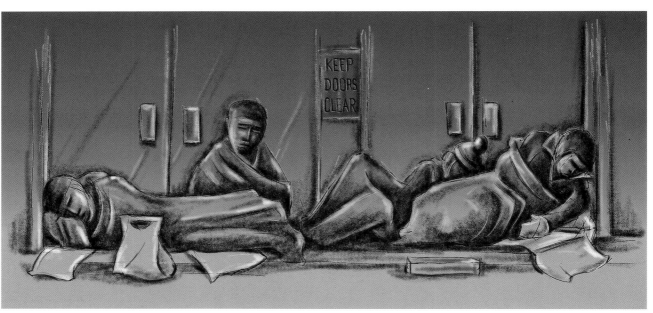

Street life

Homelessness is growing. And the people sleeping on the streets are only the tip of the iceberg. Emily Moore asks what can be done

Every night up to 2,000 homeless people in the UK sleep on the streets. The government wants to see that number cut by two-thirds by the year 2002. How can the problem be solved? Earlier this month, Louise Casey, the head of the Rough Sleepers' Unit, caused controversy by saying that giving out hot soup and sleeping bags actually encouraged people to sleep rough. Most charities agree that long-term solutions are most important, but that emergency street-based services save lives, especially in winter.

Is homelessness a big problem in the UK?

Yes. Over 10,000 people will sleep rough over the course of a year; 25% of them are aged between 18 and 25 and 90% are male. People who sleep rough are more than 50 times more likely to die from violent assault than the general population and are 35 times more likely to commit suicide. Half the people who sleep rough have a bad alcohol problem and 20% misuse drugs.

Do all homeless people sleep on the streets?

No. Street homelessness is just the tiny tip of a huge iceberg. Hundreds of thousands of people live in hostels and bed and breakfasts, or in overcrowded, damp or unsafe housing. Some of these will end up spending time sleeping on the streets.

There are around 400,000 people in England who are recognised by their local authorities as officially homeless. However, there are many more 'hidden' homeless, people who are not officially recognised as homeless. At least 41,000 people live in hostels or squats and 78,000 couples or lone parents must share accommodation because they cannot afford to set up home on their own. Centrepoint, the housing agency for young people, estimates that 200,000 to 300,000 young people in the UK (16- to 25-year-olds) are living on friends' floors, in hostels, squats or on the street.

What causes homelessness?

The homeless charity Shelter believes the underlying reason in general is lack of affordable housing and, with a boom in house prices and rents, particularly in the south-east, they worry that the problem will only get worse. People sleeping on the street are the most visible face of homelessness and have the most extreme problems. Street homelessness can be caused by family breakdown, domestic violence, drug or alcohol problems and mental illness. Family breakdown is cited by 38% of homeless people as the key factor that first drove them to sleep rough. According to surveys, only one in five of those who sleep rough do so by choice.

Most people sleeping on the streets have troubled backgrounds and need special help.

One study found that over three-quarters of homeless teenagers were either long-term non-attenders or had been excluded from school. Many homeless people have been in care and around half have been in prison. One in four have been in the armed forces.

Young people flee troubled homes and move to a new city, to find no room in a hostel and no choice but to sleep on the street. Of the young homeless, 86% have been forced to leave home. One in five

---

10,000 people will sleep rough over the course of a year; 25% of them are aged between 18 and 25 and 90% are male

---

street homeless have a serious mental health problem.

Is there a solution to street homelessness?

There are many problems and many solutions. Long-term solutions include providing more affordable, secure, good-quality housing. But handing someone the key to a council flat is not enough. The street homeless need long-term support, for example with alcohol, drug and mental health problems.

Prevention is better than cure. This means providing more support for vulnerable people before they end up on the streets. The government set up the Rough Sleepers' Unit in April. Louise Casey, head of the unit, made the headlines last week by saying soup runs and handouts encouraged people to sleep rough: 'well-meaning people are spending money servicing the problem on the streets and keeping it there'. Last week, Shelter and Crisis launched their Millennium Plus project, to provide hostel beds for street homeless people, together with advice and help at the hostel so nobody is on the streets over the millennium period. They aim also to move people off the streets for good.

The government wants to reduce street homelessness by two-thirds by 2002 and has a budget of £145m over three years to achieve this. However, it is important to remember that street homelessness is only part of a much bigger problem and that most homeless people don't live on the street, but in bad housing conditions.

- Shelter tel: 020 7336 6482, for help and advice from Shelterline 0808 800 4444
- Crisis. For information and the Crisis education pack, *Changing Lives*, tel: 020 7655 8309
- Centrepoint tel: 020 7544 5000.

© *The Guardian* November, 1999

Young runaways

Information from NCH Action for Children

Definitions

A runaway is a young person under 18 who has left home or local authority care without agreement and has stayed away for a 'significant' period of time. Included in this definition are 'throwaways' – young people who have been thrown out of their family home.

The definition is less clear once young people are over 16. In England and Wales, parents have the right to refuse to allow a son or daughter to leave home. However, this right is difficult to enforce. Once over 16 a young person may be a runaway or homeless. In Scotland a 16-year-old can leave home legally without their parent's consent.

Estimates

Based on reports made to the police, it is estimated that some 43,000 young people run-away. However, exact calculations are difficult as figures on runaways are not held centrally. Each of the 51 police forces in Great Britain maintains its own records and has its own statistical procedures. Additionally, evidence from direct work with runaways suggests many are not reported as missing.

Research questioning young people on their running away behaviour indicates that up to one in seven under-16s run away overnight and that over 10,000 of today's children will run away ten times or more before they reach their sixteenth birthday.[1]

A recent study of young homeless people found that one-third had first left home before they were 16 years old.[2]

The Children Act 1989 made the provision of refuge for young runaways a legal possibility and much of the evidence concerning young runaways is from research on young people in contact with the small number of refuges and outreach projects in existence. This suggests that the majority of runaways (68%)

are aged 14 to 16.[3] However, around 7% are 11 or younger.[4]

The gender ratio of young runaways varies slightly in different studies but overall is roughly equal. However, amongst younger runaways there is a greater proportion of boys. Young people run away from all regions, rural and urban, but much higher numbers come from areas of disadvantage.

Although Afro-Caribbeans seem to be over-represented amongst young runaways, this does not necessarily mean that more actually run away. It could be that higher numbers are reported, that people of Afro-Caribbean origin are more likely to live in areas of multiple deprivation, or because the Afro-Caribbean population has a greater proportion of young people than the national average.

Most young people who run away do so for only a short period of time. Only a quarter run away for

more than 48 hours, and only 2% for over 14 days.[3] There is a general misconception that young people invariably run away to London but research shows otherwise.[3] Most tend to stay in their home areas, although evidence suggests that if young people continue to run away, they will go further afield.

Although less than 1% of under-18s are in local authority care, studies of young runaways consistently show that at least a third have run from care.[3, 5] However, most young people (90%) start running away from home. Around 20% of these later go into, and continue to run from, care. Around 10% of all young runaways first run from care.[3]

Reasons for running away

Young people run away for a variety of reasons. Many cite problems at home such as constant arguments or a breakdown in communication with parents. Divorce and parental

Reasons for leaving home

Reason for leaving home	Number of young people	%
Serious household friction	78	49
Eviction	55	34
Relationship breakdown with family	29	18
Left local authority care	23	14
Step parent/reconstituted family	26	16
Serious lifestyle clash	11	7
To seek accommodation	9	6
Abuse (within family)	8	5
Overcrowding	7	4
Family breakup (divorce/separation)	5	3
To take up employment	3	2
Harassment	3	2
To further education	2	1
Abuse (outwith family)	2	1
Bereavement	2	1
Abandonment	1	1

Note: Details were available for 160 young people, some of whom gave more than one reason. The number displayed therefore sum to more than 160 and the percetnages total more than one hundred.

Source: Bridges One Door Project

separation often cause young people a lot of pain and lead to some feeling rejected by, or mistrustful of, their parents. For some, problems at home are extreme and include emotional and sexual abuse. Violence at home, including domestic violence, is one of the most commonly cited reasons for running away from home.

Reasons given for running from care tend to centre around frustration with the care system. Young people report feeling that decisions were being made about their future without their involvement, or that rules and regulations were imposed on them without reason. Some young people ran from care back to previous placements, or to friends or family. Worryingly, some ran from bullying by other children. Recent investigations of organised abuse in children's homes have also revealed that some victims of abuse had tried to run away but had been returned.

Other reasons cited include problems at school such as bullying, pressure to succeed, and conflict or harassment over sexual orientation.

Whilst there may be a variety of factors which precipitate running away, pervasive factors in the lives of young runaways are disruption due to family breakdown and periods in substitute care. A recent study identified a number of characteristics prevalent amongst runaways:
- at least 60% had lived in a family where a split had occurred and around a quarter had lived in a reconstituted family;
- 70% had lived in substitute care, including children's homes, foster care and secure units, with an average of 5 placements each.

Young people report some positive aspects of running away such as having time to think, and relief from pressure. Whilst running away may be perceived by adults as irrational, it is often a logical response by young people to what they feel are intolerable situations at home or in care. However, the negative effects and risks of running away far outweigh the positives. Research shows that:
- over two-fifths had been frightened whilst on the run;
- a quarter had been physically hurt;

- one in nine had been sexually assaulted.

Most young people had been hungry or thirsty whilst away, and this had led to various survival strategies:
- over half had stolen or shoplifted whilst on the run;
- one in seven had sex for money;
- others resorted to begging.[4]

Research reveals the negative impact on the health and welfare of young people:
- over a third reported trying to harm themselves by slitting their wrists, taking an overdose or attempting to hang themselves;
- over half had taken drugs;
- half reported experiencing depression.[4]

Running away and homelessness

There are also longer-term implications that arise from running away, especially in the case of persistent runaways who comprise around 9% of the runaway population[3] or, according to some estimates, 2% of the total population of young people.[1] Some persistent young runaways become detached from society. There are instances of runaways spending periods of six months or more detached from family and substitute care before the age of 16. Relying on friends and acquaintances to survive, they sleep in a variety of places including the street, empty properties or 'all night venues'. They have little or no contact with formal agencies such as social services, or with their families or the education system, all of which are key in preparing young people for the transition to adulthood.

There is a link between such detachment and later homelessness. Persistent runaways have many of those characteristics which make young people vulnerable to homelessness. Their education is likely to have been disrupted, and they may have ceased attending school, resulting in poor or no educational attainment. They are therefore unlikely to have a job and the money to secure accommodation for themselves.

In addition, because of their detachment they are less likely than other young people to have access to support networks which could help.

There is also some evidence to suggest that detached young people will not use hostels and nightshelters because of the rules which they operate. Often hostels are the first step towards resettlement.

A recent survey of young homeless people in London found that they had commonly first left home before age 16.[2]

All the available evidence shows that many runaways place themselves at extreme risk of personal harm. The outcome for those who continue to run away is often bleak. At present the only refuges are funded by voluntary organisations, there are very few of them and it is inevitable that for every very vulnerable young person they help, many more slip through the net and become detached from society.

References
1 Rees, G., *Hidden Truths: Young people's experiences of running away*, The Children's Society, 1993.
2 Brugel, I., and Smith, J., *Who is at risk of becoming homeless? An analysis of risks for young Londoners in summer 1998*, Southbank University 1999.
3 Abrahams, C., and Mungall, R., *Runaways: Exploding the Myths*, NCH Action For Children, 1992.
4 Stein, M., Rees, G., Frost, N., *Running the Risk: Young people on the streets of Britain today*, The Children's Society, 1994.
5 Newman, C., *Young Runaways: Findings from Britain's first safe house*, The Children's Society, 1989.

Running away is never the answer

Advice for young people

Around 43,000 young people run away every year for a whole variety of reasons:

'No one ever listens to me.'

'There's just no one I can talk to.'

'They won't let me stay out late with my friends.'

'They bully me at school.'

'I'm terrified they'll find out I'm on drugs.'

'I can't stand this abuse any more.'

Running away is never the answer

Whatever your problem the one thing you need to know is that running away is never the answer. It won't make your problems go away, and it will probably just make them worse.

So what can I do about it?

If you have a problem you need to talk to someone who can help. If you can, start by talking to your parents or carer. Tell them that you are worried or upset and want to talk to them about it. Try to be as calm as you can and explain what is bothering you.

Be prepared to look at things from their point of view too. Arguments over things like staying out late can be resolved. On the one hand, you need to understand that your parents are probably worried about you getting home safely. On the other hand they need to understand that you are growing up and want to be more independent.

If you really are desperate

If your situation is so distressing that you genuinely feel you cannot talk to your parents or carers then please seek help outside the family before you consider running away. The following people should be able to help:

- School teachers
- Youth workers
- GPs
- Check in the phone book or with the Citizens' Advice Bureau to see if there is a Local Youth Counselling Service
- Childline
- NSPCC

If you wish these people may be able to keep what you tell them confidential but that does depend on the problem. Check this out with them first.

Running away won't make your problems go away, and it will probably just make them worse

---

Life on the streets is frightening and dangerous

There's nothing glamorous about life on the streets. It is cold, dirty and very dangerous. You will probably be hungry, cold and scared. Don't let your problems reach the point where running away feels like the only solution. Talk to someone about your worries and get some help now.

Helplines

NSPCC: 0800 800 500
Missing Persons Helpline: 0500 700 700
Message Home: 0800 700 740
Childline: 0800 1111
Samaritans: 0345 909090

The Children's Society runs streetwork and refuge projects in Birmingham, Leeds, Manchester, and Newport in South Wales. We work with children and young people who have run away from home and care and are at risk on the streets, with the aim of sorting out their problems and returning them home or to a place of safety.

© The Children's Society

Beyond alms reach

Scroungers or victims? A global rise in the number of beggars has left policy-makers and the public equally torn about how to deal with them. Hartley Dean on new research into an ancient problem

Begging is back. In Britain, as in most of the western world, the ancient practice of asking passers-by for money seems to be on the increase as a consequence of widening social inequality and shrinking welfare support. And the dilemma for policy-makers is: should we aim to protect beggars or control them?

Society has always been ambivalent towards begging. In the past, beggars have included both ascetic pilgrims and lawless wanderers looked upon, respectively, as deserving objects of pity or undeserving scroungers. Today, the image of the beggar is equally equivocal and triggers equally strong reactions. Is he or she the hapless victim of a failing welfare state or the venal representative of an emerging underclass?

In one sense, modern social policy developed as a response to begging. The poor laws, and later the welfare state, have entailed the systematic regulation of benefits and services for the destitute and the administration of funds that had once been given to beggars as alms.

Some of the regulatory processes and administrative techniques of the 20th-century welfare state can be traced back to the criteria by which the burghers of late medieval cities began to distinguish between those 'deserving' beggars, to whom relief might be given, and the 'undeserving' beggars, to whom it should not.

However, 400 years of regulation have failed to stamp out begging. The evidence suggests that recent changes in social security, housing and provision of mental health care have actually exacerbated the extent of begging on Britain's streets. Partly because we have become accustomed to the way in which we give to meet the needs of others through the machinery of the state's tax and benefit system, there

is something discomfiting about the face-to-face contact that is entailed between the beggar and the passer-by. For the passer-by, it can be irksome to be forced to make on-the-spot judgments about whether to give or not.

More than this, the public spectacle of the beggar may expose us to a glimpse of misery we would prefer to ignore. However submissive, the beggar confronts us with the gross inequalities of the society we inhabit and the hazards to which we might any of us become subject. In the era of information technology and rapid mobility, the real and immobile presence of the beggar provides an arresting contradiction.

The re-emergence of begging is associated with global economic trends and is evident in most western cities – dramatically so in the post-communist countries of central and eastern Europe. The process of economic globalisation has resulted in rapidly increasing social inequality in several parts of the world and a

reduction in the capacity – or the willingness – of nation states to pursue protectionist welfare policies. As capital becomes increasingly mobile, and labour markets increasingly polarised, many economies have witnessed a significant growth in peripheral and informal economic activity.

Begging may be understood as just one of a range of survival strategies pursued by marginalised labour around the world – from informal employment or unlicensed street-trading at one end of the spectrum, to burglary or robbery at the other.

Meanwhile, the world's political leaders speak of ending welfare as we know it, or of reforming welfare to promote 'opportunity not dependence'. Their concern is less with social inequality than with social exclusion. Beggars, by implication, are not victims of poverty so much as extreme examples of failure to participate.

Former Conservative prime

Is kindness in decline?

A more canny Britain

- The number of people approached by someone begging in a public place has risen dramatically from 25% in 1989 to 59% in 1999. In London the figure was 80%; in Yorkshire and the Humber it was 70%.
- 62% of those who had been approached gave nothing to beggars, but 73% overall say they gave money to charity.
- Half the public now agree that many of those on State benefit do not genuinely need such help, an increase of 16 percentage points on 1989.
- 88% feel that people should be encouraged to stand on their own two feet.
- 63% dreamt about winning the Lottery at least once a month. Such fantasies are most prevalent in the East Midlands – 74% – and least so in London – 55%.

• MORI interviewed a representative quota sample of 1,979 adults aged 15+ in 160 sampling points throughout Great Britain. Interviews were conducted face-to-face, in-home, between 10 and 13 September 1999. Data have been weighted to the national profile.

© Market & Opinion Research International (MORI)
January, 2000

minister John Major, who once condemned beggars as 'an eyesore', urged that 'society needs to condemn a little more and understand a little less'. For New Labour, Tony Blair and home secretary Jack Straw have been equally quick to condemn 'aggressive begging' as 'an affront . . . to compassionate citizens' and to flirt with the idea of 'zero tolerance' policing as a means to control it.

However, if we prefer to understand before we condemn, what does recent research tell us about contemporary begging and the people who engage in it?

Much of the available research has focused on street homelessness, rather than begging. But, in some countries, begging by travellers and refugees can be just as significant as begging by the street homeless. Even in Britain, where there is a strong association between street homelessness and begging, not all beggars by any means are homeless.

Exploratory research in England and Scotland, addressing begging as a street-level economic activity, suggests two major findings. First, those who beg have generally experienced a disrupted family background, substance abuse, exclusion from the labour market and institutionalisation, in children's homes, mental hospitals or prison – or usually a combination of these factors.

Second, begging is by and large an extremely hazardous and un-rewarding occupation. Some beggars may well conform to the stereotype of the popular imagination and are supplementing income from a variety of other sources in order to sustain an expensive drug or alcohol habit.

However, the sheer diversity, chaos and tragedy that characterise the life stories of those who may be found begging on Britain's streets surpass the imaginable. While some beggars are ostensibly managing to achieve substantial 'takings' from begging, the proceeds attained by others are pitifully small. Either way, beggars are vulnerable to abuse, predation and physical violence both from passers-by and at the hands of other street-people.

Without question, many of the people who beg are very difficult to help. But this should not obscure the highly pertinent challenge which the resurgence of begging now poses for social policy-makers. In practice, it would seem that attempts to sweep beggars off the streets are likely to be wholly ineffectual unless something is done about the extreme poverty and the failures of our social institutions that are invariably associated with begging in the first place.

© The Guardian
September, 1999

Sympathy goes begging in tougher Britain

By Steve Doughty, Social Affairs Correspondent

Six out of ten people have been accosted by beggars at one time or another, it was revealed yesterday. A decade ago the figure was only 25 per cent. But pleas from the poor usually fall on deaf ears.

Nearly two-thirds of people say they give nothing to those begging in public, a survey showed yesterday.

Lack of sympathy for the less well-off is just one example of how attitudes have hardened over the last ten years, say researchers.

A huge majority of Britons – 88 per cent – now accepts the idea that everybody should be encouraged to 'stand on their own two feet'.

The research, for *Reader's Digest* magazine, shows that half the population believes that many of those living on state benefits do not really need them. Ten years ago only a third thought so.

The shrinking of the welfare state has accompanied the growth of this harder stance. But a majority of those questioned put the changing attitudes down to falling moral values and the decline of the family.

Half the population now believe the breakdown of traditional family life is responsible for making Britons a less sympathetic race. This is up ten points on a decade ago.

An even higher proportion – 56 per cent – cite a decline in moral standards, 11 per cent up on 1989. More than four out of ten, 43 per cent, think the cause is a growth in materialism, and six out of ten think a lack of discipline by parents is a cause, up five points on ten years ago.

By contrast, only four out of ten blame the influence of television, a figure barely altered from 1989. And as the performance of schools improves under pressure from governments, fewer people blame falling educa-tional standards for problems.

Only a quarter now believe poor schooling is to blame, against more than a third ten years ago. The survey also found that two-thirds of the population regularly dreams of winning the lottery.

Reader's Digest editor Russell Twisk said: 'This paints a realistic picture of life at the end of the millennium. We selfishly dream of the lottery and expect people to look after themselves.

'But there are encouraging signs for the future.

'More than a fifth of people questioned did voluntary work and we give generously to charity.

'Perhaps it is simply that we are caring, but we are canny too.'

The findings come in a poll of nearly 2,000 carried out for the magazine by MORI to see how views have changed since a similar exercise ten years ago.

© The Daily Mail
December, 1999

Can we end the plight of homelessness?

By Peter Foster

Tony Blair has pledged £200 million to end Britain's 'shame' at seeing out the 20th century with people sleeping on the streets. *The Telegraph* yesterday asked homeless charities about the difficulties in integrating back into society the 1,600 people who live rough in England.

Who are the homeless?

Homeless people can be divided into three frequently overlapping categories, according to Crisis. Neil Churchill, a strategist with the charity, said: 'There are those from abusive or broken families, those suffering mental health problems and those who have left institutional environments like care homes, the armed forces or prisons.'

Why are they homeless?

Everyone has personal stories to tell but all share the experience of being repeatedly rejected by society. Robert Black, of the English Churches' Housing Group in London, says: 'Drug and alcohol abuse or mental health problems make many of these people extremely difficult to live with. They have probably exhausted all possibilities with friends, family or hostels and simply have nowhere else to go.'

True or false? Many people are homeless because they choose to live that way.

Some homeless people do prefer the familiarity of the street culture to a bed in a strictly-regulated hostel or a lonely council flat but, given the right support, most would prefer to come in from the cold, says Mick Carroll, policy director at St Mungo's, London's largest homeless charity. He added: 'In the past, hostels which were often closed during the day had a bad reputation among the homeless. We need to attract people off the street so we can start helping them with their difficulties which is why Mungo's hostels don't have oppressive rules such as curfews and searches.'

Are there enough hostel places?

No, which is why homeless charities, particularly the hardest-pressed working in central London, welcomed the announcement of 5,000 more beds for England's homeless. Chris Holmes, director of Shelter, said: 'There are 3,000 beds in London but, at the moment, we only have two available and they are restricted to single men aged 16-25. We receive hundreds of calls every day but all the beds are usually filled by 9am.'

Will more hostel places solve the problem?

Only in the short term. All charities contacted by *The Telegraph* yesterday complained that hostels were suffering from a lack of accommodation for residents to move on to. Robert Black, of English Churches, which specialises in long-term rehabilitation of the homeless, said: 'In the long term we need to resettle these people and give them support over a period of time.'

Sister Bridie Dowd, director of the Passage day centre in London which is one of *The Daily Telegraph's* Christmas charities, agreed: 'Bringing someone off the street and back into society is a long process. Homeless people need to be given a sense of purpose and an occupation, even if

'Finding accommodation is only a fraction of the problem'

that doesn't mean employment. Finding accommodation is only a fraction of the problem.'

Do soup runs and charity handouts only serve to perpetuate homelessness?

Policy makers agree that tackling the root causes of homelessness must be the primary target of new resources, but charities who seek to alleviate the symptoms by offering hot soup and blankets still have a role to play. Mr Churchill suggests that his Fair Share scheme which takes out-of-date food from supermarkets to give to the homeless is a good compromise. 'The primary aim must be to get people off the streets, which is why we only distribute the food in our hostels to try to entice people in.'

Should you give money to beggars?

Most charities would prefer you to give your money directly to them but agree it is a matter for individual conscience. Paul Morrish, the homeless and rough-sleepers co-ordinator at Cambridge City Council, says we should not worry too much about funding the odd can of extra-strength lager. 'I give to beggars from time to time and don't worry if they will spend it on drink. After all, I spend my salary how I want to.'

Is the end of homelessness now in sight?

Depends who you believe. Crisis has set itself the goal of cutting homeless numbers by two-thirds in two years. Mr Carroll, of St Mungo's, argues: 'We should accept that some people will always be homeless. For some, the prospect of living in a flat in isolation is more than they can endure. Some people will always be moving around the circuit and we must not write them off.'

Shelterline

Information from Shelter – Scotland

It's 3 o'clock in the morning. You have 2 children under 5 and you are all crammed into a phone box with nothing. Shelter's Housing Aid Centres are closed. The Citizens Advice Bureaux are closed. You are too frightened of your violent partner to return home. Your children are cold and scared – so are you. Where can you go for help?

In December 1998, Shelter launched Shelterline, our free, 24 house, national phone line. People ringing Shelterline at any time of the night or day will be connected to a Shelter advisor who will talk through their situation and discuss their rights and options.

They can provide immediate help by telling people in crisis what hostels, projects and other services are open. They can also provide longer-term help by referring people to the closest Housing Aid Centre for more in-depth and sustained guidance and support.

Prior to the launch of Shelterline, many Scots found it impossible to get free and accurate housing advice. For the lucky few who did, it was often found too late to save their home. A survey carried out for Shelter before Shelterline, showed that in almost 40% of cases people with housing problems, the crisis could have been avoided if they had managed to get help earlier.

Shelterline means that people in rural areas, those who live some distance from our Housing Aid Centres, people who are in-capacitated or scared to leave their home, or people with problems outside office hours are now only a free phone call away from help. Help that may well prevent them from finding themselves out on the streets.

For some people, the solution to their housing problem is very simple – a decent home. For others, the situation is more complex.

Shelter Scotland could see through our housing aid work that some families found it difficult to move from temporary accommodation and settle into permanent accommodation. The Families Project was set up in December 1998 to support vulnerable families and help prevent them from becoming homeless again.

Local authorities often have a duty to re-house homeless families, but their responsibilities end when a new house is provided. After months of waiting, a family is handed the keys to their new front door and left to fend for themselves. They may be miles from relatives, friends and community. They often have no furniture or carpets, or money to buy them. They will have been through the trauma of losing their home and findings themselves in temporary accommodations. They may have fled domestic violence and have little than the clothes they are wearing.

Homeless families need help to support them to rebuild their lives. The Families Project offers

practical help and support for families moving from temporary to permanent accommodation. This can range from negotiating with the local council on the family's behalf, helping to furnish and decorate the new home to providing support to help families to regain their confidence, The project also works with the local Shelter Housing Aid Centre to ensure that the family gets all the help and advice it needs.

Unique to the Families Project are our Child Support Workers who help children cope with the distressing effects that homelessness has on their self-esteem, schooling and relationships with friends and family.

The Families Project was initially funded through the National Lottery Charities Board. However, since the project started, we have received additional help from Lloyds-TSB and Sir Hugh Fraser's Trust, amongst others, which has allowed us to extend the much-needed child support service.

Shelter runs Housing Aid Centres in Aberdeen, Glasgow, Dundee and Edinburgh. We also help to fund centres in Ayr and Lochaber. Shelter is the only organisation which provides expert, confidential and free housing advice throughout Scotland.

Housing aid is the single biggest thing that Shelter does. So what is it?

It is whatever is needed by people with housing problems.

Shelter believes that prevention is better than cure. Much of our housing aid work focuses on working with people before they become homeless, as soon as it becomes clear that they have a problem. The earlier we are involved, the greater the likelihood that we can help people to stay in their homes.

Every person is different and every problem must be solved in a different way. Shelter's housing aid workers are there to help when everyone else have turned their backs. We help to keep people in their homes and help families stay together.

Housing aid is about finding solutions to people's housing problems, preventing homelessness and enforcing people's housing rights. It can be:
- advising on a homeless person's rights to housing;
- explaining the laws that enable a tenant to remain is her/his home without being harassed by the landlord;
- ensuring that people receive their correct benefit entitlement to help them pay their rent;
- liaise with other organisations who can offer help;
- represent clients in dealings with landlords, local authorities, and housing benefit staff

or organising a reasonable mortgage repayment package to stop a family from having their home repossessed.

Our Housing Aid Centres now also take referrals from Shelterline, providing in-depth help and advice to people who have turned to Shelter when no-one else was willing or able to help.

- Shelterline: 0808 800 4444.

© Shelter – Scotland

5,000 beds to ease plight of homeless

By Cherry Norton, Social Affairs Correspondent

Tony Blair pledged to help people 'come in from the cold' yesterday as he unveiled new plans to stop people sleeping on the country's streets.

The Prime Minister, during a visit last night to a centre for the homeless near Trafalgar Square in London, announced the provision of 5,000 new beds for the homeless in England, including 550 in London. Money will also be spent training 60 specialists to help rough sleepers with alcohol, drug or mental health problems, as well as showing prisoners how to fill in benefit forms so that they do not end up on the streets when released. 'On the eve of the 21st century, it is a scandal that there are still people sleeping rough on our streets,' Mr Blair said. 'Some of our most socially excluded have been discarded in doorways for years. Now is the time to help them come in from the cold.'

The initiatives are part of the 'tough love' stance that the Govern-ment has adopted towards homeless people.

Louise Casey, the head of the Government's Rough Sleeper Unit who has criticised soup runs as validating homelessness, dismissed the idea that some people preferred homelessness. 'It is a blood awful life, both dangerous and damaging. People do not aspire to it,' she said. 'I just don't think that the people

we are concerned about are lying there because they want to. I don't accept that.'

In England around 1,600 people sleep on the streets, 635 of whom are in London. The figure, however, has fallen by 10 per cent since last year, according to Government statistics. The highest concentration in London is in Westminster, which has 234 people regularly sleeping rough. Outside London, Oxford has the most people living on the streets – 52.

The £200m that will be spent on beds, improving hostels and funding specialist workers over the next three years is money that has already been announced as part of existing Government packages.

In England around 1,600 people sleep on the streets, 635 of whom are in London. The figure, however, has fallen by 10 per cent since last year, according to Government statistics

'Ministers say they are putting more money towards helping the homeless, but they are just recycling and reannouncing existing funding yet again,' said John Redwood, the shadow Secretary of State for Environment, Transport and the Regions. 'Tony Blair promised that Labour "would do everything in our power to end the scandal of homelessness". But the Government's own figures show that they are making 3,500 more families homeless each year. This is another great Labour lie.'

Ms Casey said the Govern-ment was trying to reach the most vulnerable people and help them rebuild their lives. She said: 'We have to give people an aspiration beyond a cardboard box. At the moment when we put people in a hostel that seems to be the end solution. Charities and the Government want to help those people put their lives together and get into education, training and employment and that is the thrust of the new strategy.'

Homeless charities welcomed the proposals, but said that more preventative work was needed. Shaks Gosh, chief executive of Shelter, said: 'Ten out of 10 for helping people off the street, but I'm afraid it's only five out of 10 for stopping people from becoming homeless in the first place.'

© The Independent December, 1999

31

Rough sleeping

The Government's strategy

A top priority for the new Government when it came into office in May 1997 was to offer a fresh chance to the most excluded members of our community. And there is no doubt that among the most vulnerable of these are the people who sleep rough each night on our streets. In recognition of this the Prime Minister asked the Social Exclusion Unit (SEU) to make its first task a study of rough sleeping. The SEU report, published in July 1998, recommended the setting up of the Rough Sleepers Unit, with the target of reducing rough sleeping in England to as near zero as possible, and by at least two-thirds, by 2002.

This strategy builds on the analysis and findings of the SEU report, and puts into action its recommendations. It marks a change in the way Government tackles rough sleeping. The strategy reflects a further six months of discussions and consultations with a wide range of individuals and organisations, including rough sleepers themselves. It delivers a new joined-up approach which, building on the excellent work that the voluntary sector, local authorities and others have begun, aims to develop and focus efforts, to give the key organisations new tools to do their job, and to promote a constructive partnership approach to tackling rough sleeping and its causes. The result will be a better deal for rough sleepers, and better value for the taxpayer.

Background

Since 1990, Government has spent over £250 million through the Rough Sleepers Initiative alone on services to help rough sleepers off the streets. This money has funded outreach and resettlement work, around 1,300 hostel places and 3,500 units of permanent accommodation. There are still, however, around 1,600 people sleeping out on the streets of England on any one night. In London alone, where the majority of this money has been spent, there are some 635 people sleeping rough on any one night. A large number of these are part of a steady population of long-term rough sleepers who have not been helped effectively by previous initiatives. Therefore a new, braver approach is needed: it is neither realistic nor sufficient simply to rely on increasing the number of hostel beds. We need to do more. We need to change our approach. The balance in the system must be tipped towards the most vulnerable rather than making the streets a fast track for the most able.

In the past, Government has not adequately addressed the reasons why people sleep on the streets, and how to prevent the problem occurring in the first place. Some services have in practice sustained people in a street lifestyle, rather than helping them off the streets. Moreover, daytime street culture has become an increasing problem. Some services funded through previous Rough Sleepers Initiatives, including hostels, daycentres and permanent accommodation, have not been tightly focused on rough sleepers, and places have been taken up by others, such as daytime street users and the wider population. Responsibility for services has often been fragmented between a number of different organisations – statutory and voluntary – with a wide range of objectives. We have not concentrated enough on long-term and sustainable solutions, nor have we been discerning enough in offering help to those who most need it. We have not focused effectively on occupation for people. The result has often been that human beings have fallen through the intended safety net of support.

The Government has given the Rough Sleepers Unit a very clear remit to focus its energies and resources on offering help to rough sleepers, in particular those whom previous initiatives have not succeeded in helping. We believe that people should not in the 21st century have to sleep on the streets, and that the most vulnerable among them need our help, and sometimes specialist support, to give them a lasting solution.

The reasons why people sleep rough are many and complex. But we know in broad terms that the rough sleeper population comprises:

- 75% who are over 25
- 90% who are male
- between one-quarter and one-third who have at some time been in local authority care
- 50% who are alcohol-reliant
- 20% who are drug users

- 30-50% who have a serious mental health problem
- under 5% from ethnic minorities.

This strategy recognises the complexity of need that we must respond to, and aims to offer rough sleepers options which acknowledge their atypical and frequently chaotic lifestyles. Our long-term objective is to provide services which ensure that sleeping on the streets is never the preferred option.

The key to successful delivery of the strategy will be partnership. At its most basic, this is a partnership between the taxpayer and rough sleepers themselves. But in practical terms, it means partnership between Government and those who are charged with working with rough sleepers, or who have chosen to do so: the statutory agencies, local authorities, the voluntary and volunteer sectors and the wider community such as business and the public at large.

Six key principles

In developing this strategy, we have had the following six key principles in mind:

Tackle the root causes of rough sleeping.
We need to understand what causes people to sleep rough, and prevent it from happening.

Pursue approaches which help people off the streets, and reject those which sustain a street lifestyle.
Our aim is to reduce the numbers of rough sleepers, and to do everything in our power to persuade people to come in for help.

Focus on those most in need.
We want this strategy to help those whom other initiatives have failed. There is not a bottomless pool of resources, and it is crucial therefore that we target our help on those who are least able to help themselves.

Never give up on the most vulnerable.
It is inevitable that some rough sleepers, especially those who have been on the streets for many years, will have difficulty in coming back in. They will need specialist help and support if they are to succeed.

Help rough sleepers to become active members of the community.
We need innovative and pragmatic approaches which build self-esteem, bring on talents, and help individuals to become ready for work and occupation away from the streets.

Be realistic about what we can offer those who are capable of helping themselves.
We should be using our resources to help the most vulnerable and not to provide a fast track into permanent housing for healthy and able individuals.

© Department of the Environment, Transport and the Regions (DETR)

On the scrap heap

The government wants to cut the number of people sleeping rough. But it's far more than a bricks-and-mortar problem, argues Gerard Lemos

At last, homeless people are about to have a moment in the sun of political priorities. The government has set a target of reducing rough sleeping by two-thirds by 2002. Hilary Armstrong, the minister responsible, says it's one of the government's key objectives, and £145m has been set aside over three years.

The problem is obvious, isn't it? Homeless people need a home.

But new research by Lemos & Crane for Crisis, to be launched tomorrow at an event where Louise Casey, the government's homelessness tzar, will be speaking, suggests that finding a home may not always be the most pressing problem. For many being homeless is a relationship problem – not much support and lots of bad company – not a building problem.

Leaving the army or coming out of care might lead to bad habits as well as bad company. Falling out with family and old friends might lead to drink, depression or drugs – and then the flat goes. Getting the sack makes it worse.

Becoming homeless is not a direct link of cause to effect. It is the end result of the impact of one effect on another. Twists are added, often in quick succession, leading to a downward spiral.

Going back up that spiral may become difficult or impossible: not just finding somewhere to live, but making new friends, getting back in touch with family, kicking your habit, finding a job – all that makes for a full and fulfilled life. Help might be available in supported housing, but by then you're not really homeless any more. On the street, help with all this is rarely at hand.

The housing department is supposed to help vulnerable homeless people. The idea is if you get a flat the rest will follow. But council staff are too often rude and unhelpful.

Vulnerable people are perfunctorily turned away. They are told that a temporary job or friends in the area is not enough of a 'local connection'. People are excluded for past anti-social behaviour or rent arrears – and there are no second chances. The system is ramshackle and designed to say 'no'.

In the unlikely event it says 'yes', the flat may be on a lonely, dangerous estate. Housing benefit picks up the bill, so why not keep moving? In this research, access to housing and the allocations system got a universal thumbs down from the supposed beneficiaries. 'They think we'll take anything because we're homeless,' one person said. The balance in allocations needs to be shifted decisively towards consumer choice and a transparent system. Applicants need to know about all the social housing vacancies, not just in their district, but everywhere. Why not put them on the internet? Then people can decide what they want on the basis of their own priorities, not the council's.

Frequently, there is no help for what homeless people do want – family mediation, befriending and other forms of mutual aid provided by volunteers – and what help is available will only provide what they don't want – a flat on a faraway estate. One person told us: 'I only stayed in a flat for a few months because I was sick of living in hostels but I didn't have the support to last out.'

Anyone contemplating suicide has almost certainly heard of the Samaritans. A child who is being abused will see Childline's number at school. Something similar is needed for homeless people: somewhere everyone has heard of, to call for help from professionals or volunteers – a national breakdown

service, a sort of roadside assistance from a fourth emergency service for people who are, or might become, homeless.

They may need family mediation, a befriending service or a mentor to help them get back into work. If they need health or social services, detox or rehab, or just getting a social worker and a care package, help is often patchy and inconsistent.

The government has said the framework for assessing vulnerable people's needs is a matter for local authorities' discretion. They are wrong. A consistent national approach is needed. Anyone who wants it should have their needs assessed: drugs, drink, mental health, family and social ties and housing needs. Then they need a support plan and a named key worker. Without

these assessments, planning and delivering services will continue to be *ad hoc*. Some services will be underused at the same time as huge gaps open up elsewhere.

Louise Casey has read the new report. 'This is ground-breaking stuff,' she said. 'It redefines the homelessness problem. I'm particularly interested in mutual aid and will be considering whether it will be part of our national strategy.'

She has her first chance in her action plan, to be launched in the next few weeks. Building more and more hostels isn't the solution. If the right answers are not found now, the best chance of solving homelessness for a generation will pass. Another opportunity will not come again soon.

© *The Guardian*
October , 1999

Victims of rough justice

Rough sleepers are 35 times more likely to be assaulted than the rest of us. Scott Ballintyne and Sinead Hanks look at long-term solutions

The government is due to announce today its long-awaited strategy to tackle rough sleeping, fronted by the recently appointed 'homelessness tsar', Louise Casey.

Despite the controversy she caused, Casey was right when she said recently that those who operate short-term measures, such as soup runs, are not in a position to give rough sleepers the specialist and long-term help they desperately need. But what actually is the help they need?

Over the past 12 months, the Institute for Public Policy Research has been conducting a national investigation – funded by Crisis, the national charity for single homeless people – into street homelessness and crime, focusing on rough sleepers in London, Glasgow and Swansea, and on the police who are expected to deal with it.

It is the first research of its kind and the report, *Unsafe Streets*, reveals the daily lottery of life on Britain's streets.

Little or no attention has been paid to the experiences of rough sleepers as victims of crime –

particularly as they are currently excluded from the British Crime Survey. Yet we are dealing here with unprecedented levels of victimisation. Almost four out of five rough

sleepers have been victims of crime at least once, and nearly half have been victims of assault. You are 35 times more likely to be wounded if you sleep rough, compared with the general public, but only one in five report these crimes to the police. No surprises there, one might say. Social exclusion in action.

This situation has serious long-term effects. It seems that the frequency of some offences acts as a barrier – financially or mentally – to coming off the streets, by driving someone further down into the spiral of despair and hopelessness.

But if the streets are as unsafe as they appear to be, why do people choose to sleep on them? This brings into question the whole area of hostel provision. At the very least, we need to make sure that the first step off the streets is safer than being on them. Currently, this is not always the case.

It may also mean challenging the current anti-drug/drink rules operated by many hostels. Legally, there is no reason why hostels cannot accept drug users. Although there are clearly management issues, we need a more imaginative approach to drug use to help this group of people.

Central to getting people off the streets is intervention. Understated in the debate so far has been the role of the police. Apart from outreach workers, it is the police force who come into contact most with homeless people. Some 72% of rough sleepers admit that they have shoplifted, and the overall picture is one of repeated minor offending, which invariably leads to the revolving door in and out of the criminal justice system. But enforcement does not tackle the long-term problems. In our research, the police stated that they wanted options other than arrest.

The home office should take the lead in developing a pilot 'diversion from custody' programme for rough sleepers, bringing together multi-agency services – similar to the Youth Offender teams.

For example, facilities should be provided for rough sleepers with drink and drug problems, to divert them out of police cells and into something with more appropriate support (there is currently a three- to four-month detox waiting list in London).

We need nationwide good practice guidelines on policing street homelessness, including initiatives such as inter-agency training packages. There is currently a ludicrous situation where a rough sleeper in Glasgow may be dealt with differently from one in London. The Homeless Unit in Charing Cross, London, is pioneering new initiatives in this area – not least in establishing policing that rough sleepers trust.

Self-help initiatives such as *The Big Issue* are also important. Far from being a short-term measure, we found that the city-centre joint work between Swansea police and *The Big Issue* offers emerging good practice.

Homeless vendors who were violating their code of practice were dealt with by liaison between police and *The Big Issue* – and not simply by moving them on. Self-help in some instances can underpin emerging self-policing.

Constructive interventions with rough sleepers when they are victims can not only reduce victimisation but also help them leave the streets.

The government has been brave in setting a measurable target by which rough sleeping should be reduced and has shown willingness to tackle society's problem by setting up the Social Exclusion Unit – the only example of an inter-ministry committee in Europe.

Let's not waste this opportunity and the £139m that has been given to the Rough Sleepers Unit – and still have to face the same problems years down the line.

© *The Guardian*
December, 1999

'Sweep the homeless off streets'

Charities in uproar as culture of kindness comes under attack from new government tsar

The Government's new 'homelessness tsar' last night sparked a nationwide debate about how to get Britain's homeless off the streets by calling for the culture of kindness to be swept away. She said soup runs and handouts encouraged people to sleep rough.

Calling for a radical shift in emphasis about how the homeless are treated, Louise Casey told *The Observer* charities were handing out better sleeping bags to rough sleepers than those on sale in London's best camping shops.

Her claims, which prompted a furious reaction from charity workers, come as rocketing house prices threaten to pitch people on to the streets in numbers not seen for a decade.

Casey, who was appointed head of the Rough Sleepers Unit in

By Martin Bright, Home Affairs Correspondent

February, said: 'With soup runs and other kinds of charity help, well-meaning people are spending money servicing the problem on the streets and keeping it there. Even the *Big Issue* is perpetuating the problem.'

Casey's unit will publish recommendations next month as part of proposals to reduce the number of people sleeping rough by two-thirds by 2002. At present there are thought to be around 2,000 people on the streets.

'There is a sense of belonging on the streets and a feeling of safety in numbers,' she said. 'But where there is help inside, people should not take their help on to the streets.'

The Big Issue last night reacted

angrily to suggestions that the newspaper sold by the homeless was encouraging people on to the streets: 'I'd be horrified if anyone was saying that,' said director Sally Steinton. '*The Big Issue* gives people access to a legitimate income as an alternative to begging. Many of our sellers don't even live on the streets, but in hideous hostels and bed and breakfasts.'

Bill Cochrane of the Salvation Army, which gives out clothing and sleeping bags to homeless people and plans to expand the number of soup runs it operates around the country, said: 'We have expressed our concern about the *ad hoc* nature of some soup runs because they are unreliable to those in real need. But as long as there are people out there on the streets, we will go to them.'

Casey, a former deputy director

of Shelter, said there were so many handouts being provided to homeless people around the theatreland of the Strand in London's West End that people would often give up permanent housing to return to the streets.

'There is a plethora of services on the streets. You can get a better sleeping bag on the Strand than you can buy in the camping shop Blacks.'

Her comments come the day before the launch of Millennium Plus, an initiative by homeless charities Shelter and Crisis to clear the homeless off the streets in time for the new year celebrations. The charities will set up shelters in 13 cities across the country, which will also act as counselling and advice centres. Following the lead from Casey's Rough Sleepers Unit, all help will be received inside shelters rather than on the streets.

Shelter director Chris Holmes said that the Millennium Plus scheme was recognising that street homelessness was a priority. 'It is completely unacceptable to have even 2,000 people on the streets. We have to recognise that these people have multiple problems and handouts or the key to a council house are not always the answer.'

Shelter is concerned that the housing boom, which has seen average house prices in London rise by 53 per cent in six years to nearly £150,000, will lead to further homelessness.

The high price of property means that landlords are selling up to take advantage of the boom. Last week London's night shelters were completely full by nine o'clock in the morning.

Representatives of the Association of London Government had an emergency meeting with Housing Minister Nick Raynsford last week, after homelessness in the capital rose to a record 38,000 households, and recommended an investment of £300 million a year to alleviate the problem.

Increasing numbers of people are finding refuge in other cities. London councils are rehousing people in bed and breakfasts as far away as Loughborough in Leicestershire.

In Brighton 30 new homeless people arrive every month and its shelters are now also full. Jenny Backwell of Brighton Housing Trust said the new approach of the homelessness tsar represented a worryingly brutal trend in policy towards the homeless.

'There is a growing feeling that the voluntary sector is causing the problem and is adding to the growing tolerance of homelessness culture when we are the only people who are there to help. This is completely unacceptable in a civilised society.'

© The Guardian
November, 1999

Employment and training schemes for homeless young people

Homeless young people are one of the most disadvantaged groups in the labour market. Their problems include low skills, lack of job readiness and inadequate information on suitable employment. When they do find jobs, there can be problems with sustaining employment. There is a range of specialist employment training projects for them and this study examines a variety of such schemes in London. It focuses on the experiences of the projects, the young people who use the schemes and those who do not. The research, by Geoffrey Randall and Susan Brown of Research and Information Services, found that:

- Common problems were a history of erratic school attendance, chaotic lifestyles and poor experiences of previous training schemes. Although some were highly motivated and prepared for work, others had problems with mental health and substance abuse.
- Those who were not engaging with the training or employment services on offer had even more disadvantaged backgrounds.
- The young people's housing

A key task was to encourage homeless young people to participate in schemes in order to counteract their previous poor experiences of school-ing and training

---

problems further damaged their job prospects. Those who were sleeping rough had little chance of gaining employment. Although those in hostels had better prospects, the high levels of rents and some aspects of hostel life created work disincentives. Some of those rehoused in housing association homes also faced similar disincentives because of dependence on Housing Benefit to pay high rent levels.

- A key task was to encourage homeless young people to participate in schemes in order to counteract their previous poor experiences of schooling and training.
- Current good practice included: the use of incentives to develop self-confidence and motivation; focusing on basic transferable

work skills; flexible training with intensive one-to-one tuition; and securing help with other support needs. The young people expressed high levels of satisfaction with the services provided by the projects.

- The study identifies implications for future policy and practice including: more active encouragement by hostels for their residents to engage in work or training; the development of job-support teams to provide more intensive help with finding and sustaining employment; the development of a 'job readiness index' to monitor both young people's progress towards employment and the performance of agencies; more advice on in- work benefits and the reform of benefits and hostel subsidies to improve work incentives.

- The above infomration is an extract from *Employment and training schemes for homeless young people*, a *Findings* publication (Ref 6139) produced by the Joseph Rowntree Foundation. See page 41 for address details.

Centrepoint projects

Laying down the tracks – the projects

Young people encounter a unique set of common problems. These can be solved with time, resources and effort. But if the problems are left, they can result in lifelong homelessness. Centrepoint has developed a range of projects which can tackle them head on.

Somewhere to stay

Getting young people off the streets and away from danger is still the first priority. The streets offer many temptations to young people who may be lonely, bored, inexperienced and penniless. And there are numerous unscrupulous people ready to tempt them. Many young people who have slept rough have experienced some form of drug abuse or sexual exploitation.

Centrepoint now has 14 hostels in London, one new this year. They are equipped to cater for a range of different needs, from newly homeless young people, to vulnerable young mothers and care leavers. These projects work through a combination of counselling, providing a safe place to stay and offering employment, training and leisure opportunities.

Family and friends

A quarter of homeless young people have had some experience of the care system. Others have fallen out with their families or been forced out of home. It is also proven that most have difficulty making and keeping friends. Centrepoint's expansion means that more young people in London can remain close to their friends and family by being housed locally. The charity is also working nationwide with local authorities and the Government's Social Exclusion Unit to tackle family and care problems before they lead to homelessness. Some young people have their own family to care for. The Breakspears Road project offers young mothers special accommodation and support.

Navigating the system

Simply completing the right forms to get appropriate benefits, a job and a permanent place to stay can be highly complex and time consuming. The task can seem insurmountable to many young people. All of Centrepoint's hostels are run by staff who have the knowledge to help them conquer even the most daunting of paperwork.

Confidence

Most homeless young people suffer from a lack of confidence and belief in their own ability. Many have suffered emotional and physical abuse from a young age. Often they feel they have failed at school and see little chance of a career. These problems are tackled from a number of angles and, this year, the opportunities for young people encountering Centrepoint are greater than ever before.

Money management

Poor money management, combined with poverty, has been the cause of much homelessness. Centrepoint

---

Why people leave home and become homeless

Effects (Of becoming homeless)
Laziness, Hypothermia, Theft, Depression, Crime, Ill health, Mental Health, Mental illness, No/low self-esteem, Pregnancy, Giving up home, Stress, Prostitution, Lack of confidence, Lonliness, Suicide, Drug Abuse

Why do young people become . . .

Nowhere to go	H	Nowhere to go
Lack of social skills	O	No support
Lack of benefits	M	No money
Don't know what to do	E	Literacy problems
No options	L	Scared
No friends	E	
	S	
	S	

Roots (Why young people leave home)
Kicked out, Stress from parents, Bereavement, Peer pressure, Independence, Abuse, Leaving care, Alcohol, Drugs, Further education, Family breakdown, Arguments/fighting, Relationship breakdown, Prison

Source: Centrepoint

staff help young people learn to manage their own finances. By the time they leave Centrepoint, they should have the ability to cope without falling into debt.

Independence

Centrepoint's resettlement team works hard to enable young people to move on from homelessness and settle into their own home. Whether they are care leavers, young people with a history of sleeping rough, or young people who are independent but need support accessing private rented accommodation – help is at hand.

The Refuge

The Refuge is the only registered refuge for under-16s in the south-east and currently one of just two in England. Run in partnership with the NSPCC, it provides a safe environment for children and young people to tackle the problems which made them leave their parental home or care placement. It also helps them find an appropriate solution to these problems. Refuge staff seek to return each young person to a safe place as soon as possible. This year, a new mediation service is available which enables the residents to communicate with their families with the help of an independent, trained staff member.

• The above information is from Centrepoint. See page 41 for address details.

© Centrepoint

This is YMCA housing

Information from the YMCA

The YMCA is the largest provider of accommodation for young single men and women in the country, backed up by more than 100 years' experience in housing. But things have changed a lot since we opened our first hostel in 1873.

Today, youth homelessness is rising and young people are the fastest-growing group on local authority housing waiting lists.

Rising rents, family breakdown and unemployment have all contributed to this; so has a lack of safe, secure, affordable accommodation. Today, young people face many problems.
• in 1994, more than 16% of young people were unemployed, according to the Unemployment Unit
• in 1991, one in three children lived in households with less than half the average income, compared to one in 10 in 1979
• an estimated 50,000 young people are homeless in London alone, according to Centrepoint.

Meeting changing needs

Our work has changed to meet the needs of each new generation. Our housing is open to all young people, but more and more we are providing accommodation for the unemployed, under-18s and ex-offenders, as well as students and young workers. In one sample of 500 residents:
• 88% were unemployed

• 47% had slept rough at one time or another
• 42% had been in trouble with the police.

There's a place young people can go . . .

Young people face an uncertain future. Growing numbers are turning to us for help and more and more agencies are depending on our expertise.

With 6,300 beds for young men and women aged 16 to 35 – in 70 residential centres around the country – we provide more accommodation for young single people than any other organisation in Britain.

And we are growing all the time. In 1997, we housed 7,000 young people each night.

Designed with young people in mind

Young people today want more independence, at an earlier age, so almost all our accommodation built since 1991 consists of self-catering flats and bed-sits.

Our designs reflect the need for independence. But many young people come to us lonely and vulnerable, so our housing includes communal areas to make sure young people have social contact, and staff who can provide help and advice.

To prepare young people for life on their own, a growing number of YMCAs have purpose-built 'move-on' flats – another steps towards independence.

Others run supported lodging schemes in family homes and direct access accommodation – which takes young people directly off the streets.

More than just a landlord

Putting a roof over a young person's head is not the end of our job – it's just the beginning.

We help all our residents become independent, confident adults by providing them with a stable community, emotional support and encouragement.

Our housing provides a balanced community where residents – unemployed, working and students – can learn from each other.

We have staff skilled in teaching young people about life and we have a wealth of experience in youth work, so we are uniquely able to provide housing which meets all the needs of our residents.

Breaking the 'no home, no job' cycle

Our rounded approach to caring for young people meant we were chosen by the government in 1991 to pilot 'foyers' in this country. A French idea, foyers are residential centres which:

- provide young people with a home
- help them secure training
- give them support in finding a job.

Three out of four participants in our first foyers found a job, training, or a new home. Independent research shows that residents like the way they work.

This integrated approach – which tackles the underlying causes of young people's housing problems – has taken off.

By 1997, there will be 46 YMCAs working on foyer principles around the country.

Rooted in the community

We believe that local people know best what is needed in their own communities.

Every YMCA is a charity in its

own right, run by a board of local people working closely with the local community.

New housing schemes are shaped by a partnership with the local authority, local statutory bodies, local residents and voluntary agencies.

At the same time, YMCAs work with the National Council of YMCAs, itself a registered housing association, which negotiates government grants, private finance and voluntary income on their behalf.

This unique blend of funding helps us provide accommodation ideally suited to young people, at prices which they can afford. Inclusive rents for our new housing schemes are usually less than £50 per week.

Part of a greater whole

Set up in 1844, the YMCA has grown into one of the world's biggest Christian charities.

Here in Britain we are a leading authority in youth work and one of the largest youth and community organisations in the country. We believe in helping everyone, regardless of sex, race, ability or faith, but to do this we need your help.

How you can help

Young people are our future. We often feel powerless when faced with the problems of youth homelessness, unemployment and crime – but there is a way out.

Our work shows that investing in proper housing for young people and giving them the support they need can break the depressing downward spiral of homelessness and unemployment.

We provide practical local solutions to a national problem and you, in however large or small a way, can help.

If you would like to discuss any aspect of YMCA housing, director Andrew Harris would be delighted to let you know how you can help in your area. He can be contacted at: YMCA Housing, Colman House, Station Road, Knowle, Solihull, B93 0HL. Tel. 01564 730229.

© YMCA

Tom's story

Tom, an apprentice bricklayer, left home at 17 after arguments with his father. After a brief spell staying with his girlfriend's family, he moved into Stoke-on-Trent YMCA.

'I'm lucky to have come right to the YMCA,' he said. 'You've got counselling and welfare, a lot of people your own age, your own room, everything.'

Despite going through such an unsettling time, Tom has hung on to his job and stuck with his college course. 'If I have problems, I know I can talk to someone – your problems never go outside the counselling room,' he said.

'Without this place, I'd be miserable. I'll never forget it – I'll always know there's somewhere I can go.'

Message Home

Information from the National Missing Persons Helpline

Initially set up in the 1970s by the Plymouth branch of the Mothers' Union, Message Home joined forces with the National Missing Persons Helpline in the summer of 1994. Since then it has had to take on more volunteers to handle the increased calls.

Who calls the Helpline?

The Helpline receives calls from anyone who wants to send a message home. From the young to the old; from those who have been missing for a few hours to those who have been missing for years. All callers are important to the volunteers who man the phones 24 hours a day.

How can Message Home work?

Often people who have left home or run away feel that they cannot make direct contact with their home, even to phone someone to tell them they are alive and safe. This is where the Message Home Helpline can send a message and try to open 'a line of communication'.

Message Home goes far deeper than its name suggests. The service acts as a signpost, and puts callers in touch with other organisations that can help. The Helpline deals sensitively with a variety of issues from homelessness – where volunteers will try to offer the caller a safer alternative to living on the streets – to drugs and abuse. Volunteers often try to calm very distressed callers who are feeling particularly vulnerable and alone.

Message Home gives hope

One story which helps people to understand Message Home concerns a call from an eleven-year-old boy, Peter, saying he had left home. Although he insisted that he was fine, it was apparent to us that he was feeling very angry. After chatting with him it was obvious that everything had gone wrong both at home and at school. He had been caught by his mum smoking dope and a big row had ensued. We talked to him for a while and it was agreed that the Helpline would phone his mother. He promised to call back in two minutes.

When we got through to his mother and explained why we were calling, she burst into floods of tears. They had been desperately trying to find him and his father was out on the streets looking for him. The message back was that she just wanted her son to come home. Mum excitedly wanted to call the police to let them know he had made contact but we pleaded that she keep the phone line free for Peter.

We talked to both parties several times more that morning before Peter decided he was ready to go home. On his last phone call he said to the volunteer: 'Please will you phone my mum and get her to promise not to be angry or hit me if I go home'. At 10 o'clock that night there was a message on the answerphone saying Peter was back and everything was OK.

Not all cases end in such happy circumstances, but Message Home hopes that it helps as best it can in the vital role that it plays.

If you would like to send a message home, call Message Home on Freefone 0800 700 740.

If you would like to find out more about the charity, how you can help us spread the word about Message Home, or if you would like to make a donation please call 0208 392 4550.

• The above information is produced by the National Missing Persons Helpline. See page 41 for their address details.

© National Missing Persons Helpline (NMPH)

ADDITIONAL RESOURCES

You might like to contact the following organisations for further information. Due to the increasing cost of postage, many organisations cannot respond to enquiries unless they receive a stamped, addressed envelope.

Barnardo's
Tanners Lane
Barkingside
Ilford, IG6 1QG
Tel: 020 8550 8822
Fax: 020 8551 6870
Web site: www.barnardos.org.uk
Barnardo's works with over 47,000 children, young people and their families in more than 300 projects across the country, including children affected by homelessness.

Centrepoint
Neil House
7 Whitechapel Road
London, E1 1DU
Tel: 020 7426 5300
Fax: 020 7426 5301
Web site: www.centrepoint.org.uk
Works to ensure that no young person is at risk because they do not have a safe place to stay. Produces many publications on young people leaving home and homelessness.

Frontline Housing Advice Ltd
150-154 Borough High Street
London, SE1W 1LB
Tel: 020 7407 0660
Fax: 020 7407 0661
E-mail: frontline@hostels.org.uk
Frontline is the London housing advice service set up to provide advice and support to black and minority ethnic people who are homeless or have housing problems.

Joseph Rowntree Foundation (JRF)
The Homestead
40 Water End
York, YO30 6WP
Tel: 01904 629241
Fax: 01904 620072
E-mail: infor@jrf.org.uk
Web site: www.jrf.org.uk
The Foundation is an independent, non-political body which funds programmes of research and innovative development in the fields of housing, social care and social policy.

Nacro
169 Clapham Road
London, SW9 0PU
Tel: 020 7582 6500
Fax: 020 7735 4666
E-mail: communications@nacro.org.uk
Web site: www.nacro.org.uk
Nacro's vision is a safer society, where all individuals feel they belong (and human rights and dignity are respected).

National Homeless Alliance
5-15 Cromer Street
London, WC1H 8LS
Tel: 020 7833 2071
Fax: 020 7278 6685
E-mail: nha@home-all.org.uk
Web site: www.home-all.org.uk
The National Homeless Alliance is a national membership body for organisations providing services and support to homeless people.

National Housing Federation
175 Gray's Inn Road
London, WC1X 8UP
Tel: 020 7278 6571
Fax: 020 7833 8323
E-mail: info@housing.org.uk
Web site: www.housing.org.uk
Gives aid and advice to housing associations and other charitable agencies providing housing and related services to homeless people.

National Missing Persons Helpline (NMPH)
Roebuck House
284-286 Upper Richmond Road West
London, SW14 7JE
Tel: 020 8392 4545
Fax: 020 8878 7752
E-mail: nmph.press.virgin.net
Web site: www.missingpersons.org
National Missing Persons Helpline is dedicated to supporting the families of and those who care for missing people. In particular it provides enduring and long-term support for those who require it. This is and always will remain the principal objective of the organisation.

NCH Action for Children
85 Highbury Park
London, N5 1UD
Tel: 020 7704 7000
Fax: 020 7226 2537
Web site: www.nchafc.org.uk
NCH Action For Children improves the lives of Britain's most vulnerable children and young people by providing a diverse and innovative range of services for them and their families and campaigning on their behalf.

Shelter
88 Old Street
London, EC1V 9HU
Tel: 020 7505 2000
Fax: 020 7505 2169
E-mail: info@shelter.org.uk
Web site: www.shelter.org.uk

Shelter – Scotland
Scotia Bank House
6 South Charlotte Street
Edinburgh, EH2 4HW
Tel: 0131 473 7170
Fax: 0131 473 7199
Web site: www.shelter.org.uk
Campaign for decent homes that everyone can afford. Produces publications.

The Catholic Housing Aid Society (CHAS)
209 Old Marylebone Road
London, NW1 5QT
Tel: 020 7723 7273
Fax: 020 7723 5943
E-mail: info@chasnet.demon.co.uk
Web site: www.chasnet.demon.co.uk
Provides free and independent housing advice to homeless and poorly housed people.

YMCA
640 Forest Road
London, E17 3DZ
Tel: 020 8520 5599
Fax: 020 8509 3190
Web site: www.ymca.org.uk
The YMCA is a charitable, christian organisation. They work to help young people regardless of gender, race, ability, age or faith.

INDEX

Independence Web News

Back | Forward | Home | Reload | Images | Open | Print | Find | Stop

Live Home Page | Search | Computer | Support | System

*****

Centrepoint
www.centrepoint.org.uk
Centrepoint gets young people out of boxes by providing: accommodation, security, appropriate support, training and employment, a listening culture, self-empowerment, and the information to break down myths and stereotypes. Click on their Young People button for a series of case studies and other relevant information.

Crisis
www.crisis.org.uk
Crisis is a national charity dedicated to the relief of poverty and distress among single homeless people. Their mission is to end street homelessness through practical action to help homeless people move towards a secure, sustainable home.

Resource Information Service
www.homelesspages.org.uk
Homeless Pages is a comprehensive guide to information about single homelessness in London. More than a bibliography, it provides an introduction to homelessness, plus a database of resources, including research reports, directories, training courses and web sites.

Church Action on Poverty
www.church.poverty.org.uk
Church Action on Poverty is a national charity seeking to eradicate poverty in Britain. The site includes articles, press releases and useful web links on the issue of poverty.

Scottish Council for Single Homeless
www.scsh.co.uk
SCSH is the national membership organisation in Scotland for individuals and services working with homeless people. Click on the Research Info button for key facts on homelessness in Scotland.

Shelter
www.shelter.org.uk
Click on the Housing and Homelessness button. If you are looking for information on housing and homelessness in the UK, this is a good place to start. From this section you can read the regional homelessness statistics, request Shelter Factsheets, or read about Shelter's current research. If you are looking for more detailed information, you might like to visit their Publications Section. They produce a range of books on various housing related subjects.

ACKNOWLEDGEMENTS

The publisher is grateful for permission to reproduce the following material.

While every care has been taken to trace and acknowledge copyright, the publisher tenders its apology for any accidental infringement or where copyright has proved untraceable. The publisher would be pleased to come to a suitable arrangement in any such case with the rightful owner.

Chapter One: Homelessness in the UK

Questions and answers on homelessness, © Catholic Housing Aid Society (CHAS), *Homelessness – the facts*, © National Homeless Alliance, January 2000, *Homeless households in priority need*, © Crown copyright is reproduced with the permission of the Controller of Her Majesty's Stationery Office, *Housing and homelessness in England: the facts*, © Shelter, *Homelessness in Scotland*, © Shelter – Scotland, *Homelessness costs*, © Shelter, *Growing up homeless*, © Shelter, *The effects of homelessness on children*, © Barnardo's, *Youth homelessness*, © NCH Action for Children, *Youth homelessness – some facts*, © Shelter, *Factors precipitating homelessness*, © Crown copyright is reproduced with the permission of the Controller of Her Majesty's Stationery Office, *Why are so many young people homeless?*, © Shelter, *Shortage of rural homes 'leaves young on the streets'*, © Telegraph Group Limited, London 2000, *The hidden homeless*, © Frontline, *Single homeless people*, © Shelter, *Myths about homeless people*, © Barnardo's, *Mental health and homelessness*, © Shelter, *House the homeless and cut crime*, © NACRO, *Ex-offenders*, © 2000, Resource Information Service, *Who sleeps rough?*, © Crown copyright is reproduced with the permission of the Controller of Her Majesty's Stationery Office, *Highest concentrations of rough sleepers in England*, © Crown copyright is reproduced with the permission of the Controller of Her Majesty's Stationery Office, *Rough sleepers*, © National Housing Federation, January 2000, *Street life*, © The Guardian, November 1999, *Young runaways*, © NCH Action for Children, *Reasons for leaving home*, © Bridges One Door Project, *Running away is never the answer*, © The Children's Society, *Beyond alms reach*, © The Guardian, September 1999, *Is kindness in decline?*, © Market & Opinion Research International (MORI), January 2000, *Sympathy goes begging in tougher Britain*, © The Daily Mail, December 1999.

Chapter Two: Seeking Solutions

Can we end the plight of homelessness?, © Telegraph Group Limited, London 2000, *Shelterline*, © Shelter – Scotland, *5,000 beds to ease plight of homeless*, © The Independent, December 1999, *Rough sleeping*, © Crown copyright is reproduced with the permission of the Controller of Her Majesty's Stationery Office, *On the scrap heap*, © The Guardian, October 1999, *Victims of rough justice*, © The Guardian, December 1999, *'Sweep the homeless off streets'*, © The Guardian, November 1999, *Employment and training schemes for homeless young people*, © Joseph Rowntree Foundation, *Centrepoint projects*, © Centrepoint, *Why people leave home and become homeless*, © Centrepoint, *This is YMCA housing*, © YMCA, *Message Home*, © National Missing Persons Helpline (NMPH).

Photographs and illustrations:

Pages 1, 5, 8, 17, 22, 26, 32, 40: Pumpkin House, pages 2, 7, 10, 15, 21, 30, 34, 39: Simon Kneebone.

Craig Donnellan
Cambridge
May, 2000